Tramp's Gold

Tramp's Gold

Johnny Gold

 Robson Books

First published in Great Britain in 2001 by Robson Books, 10 Blenheim Court, Brewery Road, London N7 9NY

A member of the Chrysalis Group plc

British Library Cataloguing in Publication Data
A catalogue record for this title is available from the British Library.

ISBN 1 86105 452 1

Typeset by FiSH Books, London WC1
Printed in Great Britain by Butler & Tanner Ltd., London and Frome

To my darling Pash, for putting up with me and
supporting me, and Nicky and Claire –
you have all kept me sane during the madness and have filled
my heart with love.

Acknowledgements

My thanks go to Ian Johnstone for his help in creating this book, to Jonathan Kern for helping to collate and copy the photographs, to my dear friend Sir Michael Caine for his generous foreword, and to Jackie Collins for her encouragement and friendship.

For all the members who have supported us
during all these years.

Contents

The Gentleman is a Tramp

When I first met Johnny Gold he didn't have 'A Boite To Kiss In' but he did have a friend called Oscar Lerman who owned the greatest disco I had ever been in up until that time, called The Ad Lib. This meeting in the sixties was in actual fact the beginning of Tramp, which didn't open until eight years later with a practice run at Dollys in between.

The pairing of Johnny and Oscar was perfect. Oscar was the quiet administrator, but not *that* quiet, he was after all married to Jackie Collins. Johnny Gold, on the other hand, was gregarious, charming and above all he genuinely liked people. The premises that they bought together were those of the old nightclub called The Society in Jermyn Street. There was another partner in the deal, Bill Ofner. He was the silent partner, so silent, in fact, that although I knew him quite well, I never knew he was part of the club until fifteen years after it opened.

The trick that worked with Tramp over the last thirty years was that it was a fifties nightclub that they just cleaned up; they didn't redecorate and try to make it modern or trendy, they just left it as it was. Its secret – apart from Johnny who is the main reason for its success – was that because it was never *in* fashion, it could never get dated and go *out* of fashion.

Another secret was that the member's list was tightly

controlled. No men without women so you never got the problems associated with the truly insecure. All over the world girls were being allowed in without men, but that never seemed to cause a problem – quite the reverse, whatever the reverse of that is.

In the old days it used to be the haunt of young Guards officers and assorted 'Nigels' and it is rumoured that there is a tunnel underneath the hotel opposite, where the lads used to sneak 'ladies of the night'. If it is true, it would come in handy now to avoid the paparazzi who are always present outside; the clientele is and always was loaded with celebrities of all kinds. A lot of them go there safe in the knowledge that they will be photographed coming out. In fact, if you come out and are not photographed it is either raining or your career is over.

For me Tramp was, when I was younger, a second home at night, as it was for most people of my generation who were there from the start. It was a place to go if you were lonely or a place to take someone to show that you weren't lonely. It was a place to go if you were sad (Johnny has one of the greatest shoulders to cry on in London), or a place to go and celebrate: Johnny, again, is one of the greatest hosts anywhere. Another of its secrets is that it was always a disco where you could get good simple food – I always had steak and chips in those days. It was never a restaurant where you could dance.

Another of Johnny's attributes is that he treats everybody as if they were a star, which is why stars go there and are left alone by ordinary mortals, because they all believe that they are stars too, Johnny has told them so. It is a half-lit world of glamour, beauty, noise and promise. The promise of a great night, the promise of a brief look from a beautiful woman or handsome man, the promise of a meeting that could change your life, or just the promise you make to yourself that you will come back again and you will be happy there – or Johnny will want to know why you aren't.

To sum up, I can tell you that Johnny Gold has been one of my closest friends for thirty years in or out of Tramp. I have always loved him and the club, but that also goes for a lot of people because Johnny is the club and the club is Johnny.

Sir Michael Caine CBE, 2001

Chapter One

Dawn is breaking somewhere to the west. The faint rose fingers in the sky mean that it is after five o'clock and time for bed. Max knows this, too. We are passing what is probably the world's most famous zebra crossing, the one the Beatles walked across for the cover of *Abbey Road*. On the other side of the London street lie the Abbey Road Studios, quiet and asleep like the rest of this residential area. They are easy to find: the front wall is covered in sprayed messages of love in Japanese, Egyptian and, for all I know, Eskimo, from young people who have made a pilgrimage to this shrine over the years.

At a rough guess I must have done this walk more than eight thousand times, maybe nine thousand. Max has not done nearly as many: he is my sixth dog, a fierce-looking German shepherd with a gentle heart. I say to my well-heeled neighbours that they should pay me for this nightly patrol, which keeps the St John's Wood housebreaking statistics right down. They smile indulgently.

Actually, one night one of Max's predecessors did do some apprehending. I thought somebody was going to mug me in Carlton Hill. Nobody was around and I was a long way from home. My dog had disappeared into someone's large garden and this guy, in leather jacket and jeans, jumped out from behind a parked car. He didn't speak and I had no idea what he was up to but I thought to myself: If he comes towards me, I'm just going to kick him right in the balls and worry about it later. If he's innocent it'll be tough shit. As all this was going through my mind, my dog literally leapt out from the shadows and hit him so hard that he fell over on to his back sprawled out on the pavement with the dog on top of him barking his head off.

The chap let out the most terrifying scream you've heard from a human being. I thought: My God, if this guy's innocent, he's going to sue me for God knows what! So I called the dog off. The guy jumped up and took off. I had never seen anybody run so fast in my life. I thought: The bastard – he was obviously trying to do me up. That was a great dog.

Since then we've always had German shepherds. Before that, when we were living in a flat, we had a shih-tzu called Tramp. He would not have been so effective with the mugger, being ten inches tall and weighing about as many pounds.

Whenever I met Zsa Zsa Gabor she would ask me, as many Americans do, 'How is Tramp?' And I would begin, 'Packed to the rafters...'

But she would interrupt me: 'No, darlink, your baby.'

She was besotted with shih-tzus. She used to have a pair called Genghis and Khan. She said they were named after her right breast and her left breast. Zsa Zsa was always out to shock: nothing gave her greater pleasure than to reveal intimate details of her eight husbands, not least how much money each had.

One night in the club she introduced me to Julius, her hairdresser, not a man for whom marriage seemed likely.

'Guess where he had breakfast this morning.'

'The Dorchester?' I ventured.

'Wrong, darlink. With the Queen, in the Great Hall at Windsor Castle.'

Julius was Nancy Reagan's hairdresser as well and had been doing his duty on a state visit.

But I digress. The reason I walk the dog until dawn is not for him but for me. I need to clear my head. I can understand how actors who have come off the West End stage need to wind down. So it is with me after a night at Tramp, which I rarely leave before 4 a.m. When I have a night with some stars that frequently ends with everybody dancing, jumping on tables and having fun, I can't help but get caught up in it and come home bubbling with all the excitement.

And last night was no ordinary night. We had had a very special party to celebrate three decades of Tramp. Just a few friends: Michael Douglas and Catherine Zeta Jones, Rod Stewart, Michael and Shakira Caine, Sarah Ferguson, Joan Collins, Tim Rice, Andrew and Madeleine Lloyd Webber, Shirley Bassey, Bill Wyman, Ronnie Wood, Michael Brandon and Glynis Barber, Lulu and John Freida, Des O'Connor, Errol and Jeanette Brown, Jemma Kidd, Christina Estrada, Elizabeth Hurley, Koo Stark, Tara Palmer-Tomkinson, Lady Victoria Harvey, David Furnish, Sophie Dahl, Chris and Ingrid Tarrant, Nick and Annette Mason, Michael Winner and Vanessa Perry, Richard Desmond, Tim Jeffries, Kevin Doyle and others, as they say, too numerous to mention – except my dear children, Nicky and Claire, and my wonderful wife, Jan.

If you fear this book is going to be about name-dropping, you're right. I offer no apologies: Tramp has been peopled by the biggest media names of the past thirty years, from Frank Sinatra to George Best, from the Beatles to Martine McCutcheon. And, by the end of it, you're going to hear stories about them that you wouldn't believe. But they're true.

We – the eminent London jeweller, Theo Fennell, his wife, Louise and I – decided to make the dinner in aid of the Nordoff-Robbins Music Therapy Centre, which does a brilliant job of using music to unlock the closed world of mentally ill children.

We dined on paupiette of smoked salmon with smoked haddock mousse, then beef Wellington accompanied by Château

Prieure-Lichine. They commissioned Jane Asher to bake me a birthday cake, which had the logo Tramp on it with the dates 1969–1999 and three candles. I managed to blow them out with one breath – not bad, eh?

Michael Winner got up and started to speak. For a terrible moment I thought it was to complain about the food but his speech was filled with paeans of praise too fulsome to repeat. Then Michael Caine took over and, as in his generous foreword, continued the Gold-worship.

A boy can take only so much but there was more to come. Dame Shirley Bassey rose to her feet and sang 'Happy Birthday' just for me and my club – not just mine, the club that belonged to Oscar and Bill and me, as I shall explain.

I go to Tramp every night when I am in London – and, over three decades and now two more years, that has added up to a lot of nights. My philosophy is that a club or a restaurant really works only when the focal staff are in place and, in a sense, I am captain of the ship.

Normally I restrict myself to two Scotches during the course of a six-hour evening in Tramp so I can keep an eye on the comings and goings and goings-on. And, drive home under the limit. But last night the Bisquit cognac was a little too appealing so I took a cab.

These walks are always a time for reflection and tonight is no exception. No, it *is* an exception – a special night. I only wish my partners, Oscar Lerman and Bill Ofner, had been alive to share it with me. We had some wonderful laughs together – not least the night Mama Cass, who used habitually to fall asleep on a banquette in the discotheque, was locked in and had to spend the night alone in our basement. The phones were locked, so she had no way of calling for help. The next morning the cleaners were somewhat astounded to be confronted with the substantial figure of one of the world's leading pop singers of the time.

Does memory play tricks on you? I have tried to be as honest with mine as possible, but maybe any memoir has its errors and omissions. If you are one of the latter, let me go down on my knees and apologise. Just drop a note in the Tramp suggestion book and I'll try to do my best in the paperback edition!

In the pages that follow you will read how Frank Sinatra changed the lighting at Tramp, Roger Moore and Tony Curtis mopped out the floor after we had been flooded, and Freddie Laker celebrated a triumph while he was being cruelly duped.

The Beatles and the Stones figure prominently in the early club days: Ringo had his wedding reception in my restaurant and the three remaining Beatles sang together for the first time. I'm prepared to confess to a couple of mistakes I may have made, such as delivering a near fatal packet of drugs to Peter Sellers on honeymoon in the South of France and introducing one Pamella Bordes to the then editor of the *Sunday Times*, Andrew Neil. Also the bad boys I had to ban from the club.

OK, I've chosen some of the more sensational incidents to titillate you but, in the main, it has been three decades and more of incredible fun and friendship. And it's not over yet!

However, to begin at the beginning...

Chapter Two

In early 1939 my father, Sam Gold, was convinced that war with the Germans was inevitable and that London, where we lived, was certain to be heavily bombed. So he moved his family to Brighton.

His judgment was correct in both cases. German bombers scored a direct hit on my father's millinery factory – putting him out of business. However, our ex-home in Stamford Hill in north London remained unscathed but our rented flat in Marine Gate in Brighton took a direct hit. So we lost our home and Dad's business. Our new life on the south coast did not get off to the most promising of starts.

I was born Jesse John Gold on 25 June 1932 in Stamford Hill. My parents had lived in Cable Street, a focal point for many Russian Jewish emigrants. My grandparents had been driven out of Russia by the widespread anti-Semitism in the early part of the century. My mother's father was actually a Cossack. Maybe that's why I have such a way with horses – I can't back a winner.

Both sets of grandparents came from a little village outside Kiev. I went to visit it in 2000 with my wife, Jan, to see if I would get any feeling for my roots. The trip was wonderful, but, sad to say, I had no sense of my Russian ancestry at all.

However, when I was doing my national service in Germany in

the fifties, I spoke reasonably good German, which I had learnt at school, so I was always asked to chat up girls in the bars. And one day a barman said to me, '*Du muss deutsches blut haben.*' (You must have German blood). And one or two other Germans subsequently made similar remarks, so when I got home I asked my father if I did. 'Of course you do,' he said, 'on your grandfather's side.'

We rented an apartment in a block called Marine Gate. It was there that I spent my formative years. I can remember one day my mother and the other women in the flats grabbing towels and blankets and setting off for Newhaven, which is a little port just outside Brighton. The boys were coming home from Dunkirk and all the women were rushing around and making tea and helping to look after them.

There was a quite incredible spirit of togetherness at that time. When the air-raid sirens went, I would be yanked out of bed and taken to the basement of the building, which was used as a bomb shelter. Women would come down with sandwiches and flasks of tea. There was an unbelievable atmosphere. People were not cowering in corners but laughing and joking and having a good time. Especially after the shock of Dunkirk, everybody lived their life for the day.

I had the constant feeling the Germans were pursuing me personally throughout my childhood. When I was about eight I was cycling home from school one afternoon along a narrow road by the gasworks. Suddenly, this plane came up from under the cliffs. I could see the flashes of his machine gun before I heard it. But I had no doubt he was aiming for me. One of his bullets hit the front wheel of the bicycle – totally buckling it. I just threw myself off the bike and landed in the doorway of a house. I wasn't so worried about what the German might do to me, but what my elder sister, Fay, would do. It was her bike. And I was right – when I got home I felt the end of her hockey stick.

I wasn't alone in being a target for the Luftwaffe. There were many instances of children being machine-gunned in Brighton parks. A kid I knew got half his head blown off. It seemed unnaturally barbaric behaviour by what was seen as a slightly more decent arm of Hitler's military machine. People thought it was to lower morale, but after the war books on the Luftwaffe revealed that this was the way they used to blood young pilots stationed in northern France. They would send them out over the English Channel, instructing them to fly very low to avoid enemy radar, and order them to make a hit before returning to base. Any hit.

Half of the flats in our block had been commandeered by the Royal Navy. The girls' public school, Rodean, just outside town, was turned into an officers' training college during the war. They used to come and stay at the flats at the weekend. I was one of those dreadful children who would go round asking all the officers if they had any souvenirs: buttons, badges, bits of shrapnel, empty bullet cases, any memorabilia. As soon as a new batch of officers would arrive, I'd go to their apartments.

There was a lot of excitement about this Greek prince who was due to come. When he arrived he had an imposing beard. I remember going up and asking him for souvenirs and he said, 'No, but I tell you what you can have.' And he gave me a chocolate peppermint cream sweet – something you didn't see during the war years. I was over the moon. That was Prince Philip – my first contact with royalty.

As the officers had a midnight curfew, my parents used to leave our door unlocked so that they could come in late through our apartment and climb up from our balcony to theirs. At the weekends, they used to drag my parents out of bed and ask them up to their parties. Sometimes we would have a party for them in our flat and I would be allowed to stay up. Maybe that was where I realised how much people need to enjoy themselves and relax – even during the most adverse times.

But, late one Saturday afternoon in the summer of 1940, all this came to an end. My father had gone off to the dogs. Nobody complained about that, since he usually came back in profit. I remember that it was very hot and I was in my swimming trunks, playing a game of 'You're It' with some other children in the back garden.

We heard the sound of the plane before we saw it. A Fokker Wolfe 190 swooped low over the gasworks, both machine guns blazing, and then turned its attention to us children in the garden. We automatically dashed for cover in the long grass and threw ourselves to the ground.

I was the furthest away, right against the back wall. When the plane had passed, I looked up in time to see a bomb leave a second plane and huge flames go up. I was terrified that all sorts of masonry and debris would come flying towards me, so I buried myself in the long grass as deep as I could, my body tensed up waiting for something to hit me.

The plane roared over me and at the same time came the nightmare sound of crashing rubble followed by people shouting. I remained frozen in the same position until I heard the desperate scream of a woman's voice, ordering all the kids to come in.

I got up and started to run. Then there was the sound of more machine guns and I just threw myself automatically down again, this time much closer to Marine Gate. I looked up and I could see another plane drop a bomb. I remember thinking: That seems a long way away.

But it wasn't. It was right over our block of flats. I kept my head down in the grass for what seemed like forever. Nothing happened. I thought the bomb must be a dud. I'd only raised my head for about half a second when – Boom! A great wave of glass came showering towards me.

This time our apartment block had taken a direct hit. I knew my mother and sister were in there and in a blind panic I began to run towards the building – or what remained of it – to search for them. But as I ran the other kids started to shout at me: 'Jesse, Jesse, you're dying.'

I didn't know what they were talking about. The adrenaline just kept me going. I didn't notice that I was completely covered in blood. There was a door off its hinges at the back of the building. I ran through that and up a staircase to the first floor. The landing was so dense with dust and smoke that it was impossible to continue.

So I went back down and started to run round the side of the building. But I was stopped by an ARP warden in a helmet who took me and laid me down on the grass beside a wall. I told him I had to get to see my mother and he said he was sure she was OK or something to that effect. I can't really recall because I must have conked out.

The next thing I remember was my father standing over me saying, 'Are you all right?' They'd announced at the dog track that our block had taken a direct hit, so you can imagine how he felt.

I told him I was fine. His face was white as a sheet. 'Where's your mother?' he asked.

I shook my head. 'I don't know.'

The words were hardly out of my mouth – this is God's truth – when my mother and my sister appeared round the corner. Both of them had their hair literally standing straight up because, in the blast, all the dust and powder had got into their hair and put everything up on end.

My mother had a towel round her hand and arm, covered in blood. They were lucky. When the first bomb landed they rushed to the window at the back of our apartment to see how I was. Then the next bomb hit the front wall of the garden of our block and bounced right into the basement beneath our apartment, blowing out the windows and half of the building away. My mother and sister were luckily in the other half. They were thrown to the floor and my mother put up her arms to stop a door falling on her and the handle went right through her hand, missing the nerve cord by a millimetre. It was the first time I had ever seen my father cry, albeit in relief.

I remember thinking how unreal it all seemed. I suppose today I would say surreal. We, as a family, two of us dripping blood, walked round to the back of the building. There was action everywhere. The place was now surrounded by fire engines and ambulances. They'd set up emergency operating tables on the remaining balcony. I watched as they pulled a sheet over somebody. Thirteen naval officers were killed that afternoon.

My mother and I were taken to hospital in an ambulance. They had to use a probe to get the glass out of my body. The surgeon said he counted 57 separate cuts – Gold's 57 varieties. Unfortunately, they weren't able to stitch up my foot, so I was to spend the next six months in a wheelchair. When I was being pushed around the streets of Brighton people would ask, 'Who did that to you?' And when I told them they would say, 'We'll get them for you, son, those dirty, bastard Germans.'

Ironically, my father had been rejected by the forces because of a damaged leg. He desperately wanted to get into the navy but they wouldn't have him. He had had a football accident when he was thirteen, a bad break that got worse. They nearly amputated his leg and now it looked like a map of Britain with all the stitch marks.

But my sister, Fay, joined the navy as soon as she was old enough. She was a Wren and ended up in Intelligence. She couldn't reveal what she worked at until recently because of the Official Secrets Act – it was to do with code breaking.

After we were bombed out we were temporarily put up at the Norfolk Hotel – courtesy of His Majesty's Government. It was there that I fell in love for the first time. I must have been all of eight. There were three steps going up to the dining room and I would get out of my wheelchair and hop up them. One evening I slipped and fell. Looking up, I saw this long and shapely female leg. It belonged to a beautiful girl who used to do a sort of cabaret at the hotel with another girl. Her name was Kara. She picked me up and took me into the dining room.

She asked my mother if she could take me out in my wheelchair, which she then proceeded to do most days. I was totally besotted until, one afternoon, she introduced me to this handsome Norwegian fighter pilot and told me he was her fiancé. He asked me about my foot and said, 'Don't worry, Johnny, I'll get one of those Fokker Wolfes for you.' And he must have, since he subsequently got the Distinguished Flying Cross – the DFC. But, emotionally, I was gutted.

Most of the kids I knew had been evacuated so I had nobody to play with. We could see the flashes of German guns across the Channel – that really brought the war home to you. And the beaches were out of bounds – they were mined and covered with barbed wire and barricades to repel the invasion that everybody assumed was imminent.

Everybody, that is, except my father. I can remember him saying, 'There's no way they're going to cross the Channel.' He was absolutely adamant about this and he was equally adamant that he wasn't going to move. My mother said she didn't intend to move without him and my sister said she wasn't going to leave them. And neither was I.

We did have a remarkable opportunity to take refuge in America for the duration of hostilities. It came through the Reverend Fausner, the cantor at our synagogue. He taught me my bar mitzvah and he also used to tell me about his great friend, Emanuel Goldenberg in Bucharest. In 1893, when he was ten, Emanuel emigrated to America and later won a scholarship to the American Academy of Dramatic Arts. He then went on to Broadway, where he wrote a hit comedy, *The Kibitzer*. But when it came for a move to Hollywood, Fausner told me, all Jewish actors would change their names – Jews were meant to own Hollywood studios, not appear in movies. So Emanuel Goldenberg became Edward G (for Goldenberg) Robinson and rose to fame and fortune as Little Caesar.

They used to write to each other all the time. When war was

declared, Robinson asked Reverend Fausner if he and his family would like to come and stay with them in Beverly Hills for the duration. Fausner declined – synagogues and churches in Britain were naturally greatly in demand at that time. So Edward G wrote back and asked if there was another Jewish family whom he was friendly with – 'I'd be happy to do the same for them.' Fausner came to see us and my dad said, 'That's a great idea – I won't go but my wife and children will.' You can imagine my annoyance when my mother and sister again refused to leave him. I can remember saying, 'I'll go.' However, the offer wasn't open to an eight-year-old boy.

I've often wondered what would have happened if they had said yes. Growing up in Hollywood with a star who was making films with Barbara Stanwyck like *Flesh and Fantasy* and *Double Indemnity*. My life might have turned out very differently. But it was not to be, I'm pleased to say.

At one stage I did go up to Berkhamstead, where many of my friends had been evacuated, for a week's holiday. They were on a farm. I hated it. All those cows and all that country – although I didn't mind the horses, for which I've always had an expensive affection!

I'll never forget the day I accompanied my mother to visit her parents. We were just coming out of Victoria Station when a V-1 flying bomb – a doodlebug – came over. We could see it somewhere over the Thames. You were OK as long as you could hear the drone of the doodlebug's engines – it was, in effect, an unmanned plane full of high explosive. We were no sooner out of the station than the engine on this one cut. And then there was silence. The most eerie and frightening silence.

Everything stopped. Everyone stood still and just held their breath. It was like a video with the pause button on. Nobody knew where it was going to fall. We waited like this for what seemed like minutes and then there was a huge explosion, somewhere to our left in Pimlico. Maybe it hit a deserted patch of land; maybe it hit a crowded office. We, at least, were safe. Everybody simply unfroze and went on with their journey.

In Brighton, some weeks after that, an enemy bomb hit the Kemptown Odeon. It was a Saturday morning and they were showing Hopalong Cassidy movies for kids. More than two hundred children were killed. Thinking back, one came to accept death as part of daily life. We would mourn for those who died and comfort the families who were bereaved, at the same time knowing that it may be our turn next time.

You go through childhood only once and you don't miss what you haven't had. In a way I was fortunate. If I'd been nine instead of seven when the war started I might have been accustomed to fruit. But I never saw, let alone ate, an orange or a banana or a grape. We had only home-grown apples . At the end of the war my mother said, 'I've got a surprise for you' – and it was an orange. I just looked at it – it was incredible. All food was rationed: we lived on a diet of corned beef, powdered eggs and a lot of rabbit. I never felt underfed because I didn't know any differently. I didn't know what it was to have a new toy. Any metal had to go to the war effort, so we had to make do with second-hand toys. All wartime kids grew up that way.

Nor did we have chocolate – until the Americans arrived. My sister, who was very pretty – especially in uniform (men love a girl in uniform) – used to take my hand when she walked down the street. Not for my protection, but for hers!

The Yanks used to whistle and shout at her. I suspect she rather liked it. I certainly liked the Hershey Bars the soldiers used to give me in the hope of making her acquaintance.

My father sent me to the local public school, Brighton College. Since the bombing of our flats I had developed the habit of throwing myself on the ground and putting my hands over my head at the sight of a German plane. So my mother went to see the headmaster and told him about this behaviour and asked him if they could not make any fuss about it, just pretend it didn't happen. The doctors had said that it would pass eventually, which it did. But for my first terms there I would dive under the desk every time a plane went over without even realising I had done it, and they would have to pull me out.

I decided to become a boarder at the school, although it was nearby, because I wanted to feel more part of it. I loved the place, not because of the lessons – academically I was a disaster – but because of the sport. I was, and I remain to this day, a sports freak. I was on the rugby team, the gym team, the swimming team, the cricket team. And the boxing team. One afternoon I boxed for the school against Dulwich College. Although I was fourteen, I was matched against a boy of eighteen and got a severe beating. Every time this guy connected with my face it came out in a lump, so by the time the bout was over it looked as if it had been hit by a bus.

I had arranged to go for a cup of tea with my father at a café he had a part interest in on the Brighton seafront. He was with Monsieur Eddie Grey of the Crazy Gang – the most famous comedy troupe of the time. He lived in Brighton and was a golfing chum of my father's. Eddie looked at me and said, 'I suppose you won.' Then he dropped his false teeth down – a favourite trick of his – and raised his fists, saying, 'Come on, young Gold, I'll go three rounds with you.'

I lived and breathed boxing as a child. On school holidays my father let me stay up until 3 a.m. if Joe Louis was fighting, to listen to the wireless. Dad knew many of the guys in charge of boxing in those days, including Jack Solomon. So I was able to go to the gymnasium where many of the professional boxers trained. I was taught to fight by Gus Lesnevitch, who was to become the world light-heavyweight champion. He used to train with a leather mask on because he cut quite easily. I watched him beat Freddie Mills and he became my absolute hero.

I became friendly with many boxers such as Billy Walker –

later to become a business partner – Ron Barton and Dave Charnley. To this day, I'm lost in admiration for men like these. It takes such guts to go into the ring and put yourself truly on the line against an opponent who might mash you to pieces.

Chapter Three

After the collapse of his millinery business – his factory used to manufacture women's hats – my father pretty well had to start over again. The café was one of his enterprises but he also started to build up a betting business. Most of the racecourses in England were closed down during the war – there was the danger that, in the event of an invasion, the Germans might use them as landing strips for their gliders and smaller planes. So the Home Guard put barbed wire and other obstacles across the tracks.

I do, however, remember going to Newmarket races with my father early in the war. He was a tremendous judge of horses – and of greyhounds – and, after the bomb, actually made a living from betting on them. He would sit for hours studying race cards from previous years to work out the form of dogs and would then enter his conclusions on his own special card. Over the months he made a very good profit.

He was enormously proud of his card and word of it spread. A big London bookmaker – Manny King, big both in stature and in the size of his business – heard about him and suggested they might be able to do a deal that would be financially beneficial to them both.

For some reason I was there when Manny King came down to Brighton to meet Dad. After the usual preliminaries the London bookmaker revealed that he, also, had a card and he suggested, 'Let's compare cards.'

I'll never forget the moment. My father quietly froze. 'I don't compare cards with anybody,' he said. 'We have no deal.'

He might have done well out of it but such was his pride in his own judgment that he felt insulted by anybody – however big – wanting to compare selections with him.

It seemed natural for Sam Gold to start his own bookmaking business in Brighton and that was what he did. The shop was, in fact, an SP office – SP standing for 'starting price'. My father was a commission agent. What he did was to take bets, either by phone or from people who came in, and pass them on to various bookmakers (not including Manny King!). You took a commission on each transaction so it was a less risky way of making a living.

Inevitably, I, too, became more than a little interested in horses. There was a stable, just outside town, where in return for mucking out they would let me ride their mares. There was nothing more exhilarating than galloping flat out across the Sussex Downs: I always imagined myself as a cowboy, riding the range.

I had a friend called Bertie Page, who was a keen amateur jockey. His sister, Jill Day, pert and blonde, was a well-known singer for many years. One Saturday afternoon I went with my friends to watch Bertie riding at Plumpton races. He assured us that his mount, Hannibal, had a good chance of winning but not to bet on it. Needless to say, everybody put on every penny they had in their pockets. We didn't have enough money to be in the main enclosure so we took up a position on a mound by the fourth fence to watch the race. And that was exactly where Bertie and Hannibal parted company. You never heard a jockey get such a bollocking. 'I told you not to back it,' he moaned as he picked himself up. 'Yes, but you didn't mean it,' said his sister, with exquisite female logic.

I know that, from that day, I was hooked on racing.

Although my father didn't have an on-course betting licence, he loved to go to the races, and I would often accompany him. He taught me how to do a simplified form of ticktack – the way the bookies on the rails lay off their bets by touching their nose, chin, shoulders and elbows to give signals to a partner in the stands. Each has a slightly different system, but a working knowledge of the basics can sometimes help you to find out how the last-minute money is being placed on various horses.

I had a memorable day at Sandown races when I was only fifteen. I was in the free ring, which was in the centre of the racecourse, and my father was in Tattersall's, where he could get a close look at the horses. I watched him leave the ring in great haste and rush to the rails to attract my attention. I put up my binoculars and saw him signal that I should put a pound on horse eight to win if I could get odds of 10–1 or better. The horse was called Nailor, I'll never forget that, and I found a bookie who was offering odds of 25–1. Recklessly I put on £2. The race was a five-furlong sprint and the sprint course went right through the middle of the racetrack, so I had a very good view of Nailor as he won by about three lengths. I was so excited – I nearly peed in my pants.

At the racecourses in the late forties there was a celebrated tipster called Prince Monolulu, who was as famous as any jockey with his cry of, 'I got a horse! I got a horse!' People would buy tips from him and they must have been quite good, because he stayed around for a fair number of years. But on this particular afternoon, before the last but one race, he started to shout, 'I have to tell my clientele I have made a mistake in this race. I didn't realise that [he named a horse – I don't remember what it was called] was running. If I had it would have been my selection. So this is a free public tip.'

Whether this was a clever ruse to get more clients or a genuine error, I didn't wait to find out. Flush with my £50, I placed £3 on the Prince's tip and it came home at 33–1.

I went home that day £150 richer. That was really serious money fifty years ago and I doubt whether – if I index-link it – I've had a better day at the races since. I've certainly had enough of them when the money has flowed in the opposite direction.

Racing was in my blood from that early age. I was extremely close to my father and would spend my spare time helping in his SP shop. He taught me how the business ran – how bookmakers would lay off money if too much went on one horse. He was very much into breeding. He would say that if you see a horse whose sire is a sprinter and whose dam is a sprinter you know the horse is going to be a runner – he's not going to stay over a mile or a mile and a half because his breeding shows he's only a sprinter. There are obvious exceptions, but it's amazing how frequently this is the case.

I left school just after my seventeenth birthday. It was too early to worry about a career: I knew that I would have to go into the army within the year. I resolved to spend as much of the summer of 1948 as possible on the beach. A friend had a transistor radio and we were able to listen to the Olympic Games from the White City in west London. This life was inconvenienced by the need to earn some money. Using some old contacts of my father's, I got a job selling women's hats.

Another friend, Tony Lewis, was one of the funniest men I've ever known in my life. He went on to become an agent to big stars such as Shirley Bassey and Dick Emery and, even in his retirement, he remains one of the funniest. In those days he made a living selling toilet paper, which he used to say came in three qualities: 'Soft, medium and uggh!' But he sold a lot, primarily to American bases. He drove round in a big left-hand-drive Chevrolet, which was most impressive – especially to the girls.

Tony offered to teach me the art of salesmanship and took me with him to one of the American camps. 'I'll introduce you as my Swedish paper expert – that'll impress them,' he said.

'But I don't know a thing about toilet paper,' I protested.

'Don't worry,' Tony assured me. 'I'll tell them you don't speak a word of English.'

So we drove into the camp and asked to see the quartermaster. Tony introduced me to him and said, 'This is Johann Svenkelsen, my Swedish paper expert.'

I smiled and the guy said, 'Oh, my wife's Swedish. She'd love to meet you.'

As he called her on the phone I waited for the ground to swallow me up. But, luckily, she was out shopping. The quartermaster asked us over to the sergeant's mess, where we got into a game of stud poker with Tony and me as partners. We were doing very well with me, silently, scooping up the pot and the quartermaster's partner, a beefy guy called Bruno with a crew cut, getting pissed off about this. The next round, after we had put our bets on the table, Tony finished dealing and picked up his cards. And Bruno simply scooped the money up and said, 'You lose.'

'What the hell do you mean?' Tony demanded.

'You didn't burn the pack,' Bruno replied.

The expression meant taking the top card, after you had finished dealing, and putting it face up underneath the pack so that you couldn't then deal from the bottom.

'Nobody told us those were the rules,' Tony protested.

'We don't have to tell you,' Bruno insisted: 'they're our rules.'

'Well, fuck you then,' I shouted, throwing my cards on the table and breaking out of my Swedish silence.

I don't think the toilet-roll deal went through.

For some of that year I helped my father in the SP shop but my last job was selling ballpoint pens. They were new at the time and these were a copy of Eversharp, the prototype. The guy who hired me said he wanted half a crown (12½p) for each one I sold and I could keep whatever I sold them for above that price, so I went around weighed down with pockets full of pens. I did good business: tobacconist shops, at the dogs, rugby and football matches.

Then, one day, somebody asked me, 'What about the refills?'
I told him I would have them in soon and hurriedly phoned the
guy who supplied the pens.

'What about the refills?' I asked. 'What bleedin' refills?' he
replied. It was a good thing I already had my call-up papers for
national service.

I must have had a good enough report from my headmaster –
about my sport, certainly not my academic record – to be offered
the chance of going before a War Office Selection Board. If you
were selected, you trained for a year and then you became a
second lieutenant. I declined the offer. I told the guy who was
interviewing me that I was being forced to join the army, I didn't
want to join and I wasn't going to knock my brains out for a year
just to get a pip in something I didn't want to be in.

The officer said, 'That's not the right attitude.'

I replied, 'I'm really sorry, but it's mine.'

So they asked me what I wanted to be and I said I'd like to be
a physical training instructor. They told me that involved
signing on for three years, so I changed my mind about that
pretty quickly. Given the alternatives of infantry, artillery or
armoured corps, I opted for the last, calculating it would involve
the least walking.

So I became Trooper Gold 22429378 – sir! First with the
14th/20th Hussars and later with the 6th Royal Tank Regiment. I
spent nearly all of my two years' conscription in Germany. I wasn't
fond of the country or its people to say the least after the war years.
I used to get very hot under the collar. Being a Jew who had lost
relatives in the Holocaust made my attitude pretty unforgiving.

Inevitably with such a mix of new recruits – public-school
boys, Scots, cockneys, Brummies, Geordies, the lot – there was a
certain amount of trying it on at first. One guy in particular,
Johnny Paynter from 'Oxton, seemed to take an instant
exception to me. When I opened my mouth on the first night in

barracks (I had been to a public school, remember), he called out, 'Listen to Little Lord fuckin' Fauntleroy.'

I tried to ignore him. Fatal. When I got up to go to the bathroom he shouted after me, 'Don't forget to wash behind your bleedin' ears, you poof.'

I stopped and pulled my shirt over my head. I'd spent a lot of the summer on the beach at Brighton and my body – oh, for those days – was tanned and fit and muscled from gymnastics. Somebody had even tried to enter me for Junior Mr Great Britain. But I was much shorter than Paynter, who was a barrel of a man, and I was shitting myself. You make these decisions fast. I walked over to where he was sitting on his bed, grabbed him by his shirt and growled, 'If you open your mouth one more time I'll be forced to do serious damage to you.'

He seemed stunned. I threw him on the bed and said, 'Now, do you want to have an argument about the way I talk?'

As I held my breath, trying to look cool but menacing, he said, 'No.'

So I turned and continued my walk to the washroom. The whole hut was watching. And I heard him shout after me 'Oy, oy – there he goes, the fuckin' brown Brighton bomber.'

Needless to say we later became very close friends.

The first four weeks were spent square-bashing which was tough and tedious. The fearful Sergeant Major Parneby was six foot seven tall and had a reputation that preceded him throughout the tank corps. One night he came bursting into the hut and screamed, 'Anybody in here who's got black shoes, stand in front of your bed!'

Three of us did.

'Right,' he snapped, 'you're going to be waiters at the Ramnugger Ball.'

The following night we turned up in white jackets, dressed as waiters. It was a special night in the officers' mess that commemorated one of the 14th/20th's bygone victories. Parneby was always having a go at me but I think he quite liked me. 'You – Brighton –

are going to serve at the colonel's table and you'd better fucking well behave yourself, young man. I'll be keeping my eye on you. If somebody offers you a drink you'll say "I'll have a Newcastle Brown".'

It was my first experience of working as a waiter – in fact, it was the first time I had been to a dinner dance and observed the officer class at play. They certainly knew how to enjoy themselves to the full. Without doubt, some of the seeds of my future vocation were sown that night.

But it proved thirsty work running from the kitchen to the tables and I consumed three or four Newcastle Browns, having no idea how strong they were. I was more than a little tipsy when a fairly pissed officer's girlfriend – very debutante – said, 'Come and dance with me.'

I told her I wasn't there to dance but she insisted: 'Come and dance.' She took me by the arm and pulled me on to the dance floor. I just did a few steps and, looking round, saw a red-faced Parneby looking at me.

'I'm sorry, I really do have to get back to work,' I told her, and took her, protesting, back to her place. I picked up my glass of Newcastle Brown and apologised to her officer boyfriend, who was looking none too pleased.

Back in the kitchen the lofty and very angry Parneby repeatedly banged me on the head. 'You are the lowest form of life and you do not dance with officers' girlfriends.'

I got seven days' jankers. This consisted of getting up at the crack of dawn, putting on your best pukka dress – everything highly polished down to your boots – and then rushing back to put on your denims and peel potatoes or paint white kerbstones for the rest of the day. One malicious corporal made me dig a hole that I could stand in and then told me to fill it up. I nearly hit the guy with my shovel.

I started out as technical store man, and worked in a huge room the size of half a hangar with piles of spare parts for the tanks all over the place. One day, the quartermaster came to see me and told me to expect a visit from the colonel the next day, as he was inspecting our troop.

'You'd better have everything perfectly piled and spotless, Gold,' he warned, 'or you're going to find yourself in almighty trouble.'

I didn't go to bed that night as I arranged perfect piles of everything from power packs to replacement turrets and removed every speck of dust in sight.

Colonel Henry Anthony Lascelles arrived with his inspection party at ten the next morning. He was held in awe by everybody, not only because of his high rank but because he was actually a cousin of the Queen and used to go and stay with her.

He walked around, poked at things with his swagger stick and made no comment until finally he was about to leave. As we all saluted he announced, 'This place would make a wonderful pigsty.'

The captain looked at the young second lieutenant who looked at the quartermaster, who looked venomously at me. I, in turn, looked for a convenient hole in the ground to swallow me up. I would be doing jankers for the rest of my military service. Two years of peeling potatoes.

To my surprise I heard nothing from the quartermaster that day, nor the next. Was there going to be a court martial? I ventured to ask my sergeant what my penalty was likely to be.

'For what?' he asked.

'For keeping this place like a pigsty,' I replied.

He roared with laughter. 'The colonel has a huge pig farm in England. It was a compliment.'

Relief is too small a word to describe my emotions. I suppose I was sufficient of a rebel, however, to find myself doing many jankers. But, to my surprise, I had a great time in the army. Much of it was like an extension of school. I played rugby for my regiment, and boxed and did athletics and gymnastics. If you were a sporty chap, you used to get away with murder.

*

Having started out as a technical store man, I trained as a driver and got the best job of all. I had my own scout car and I would go around looking after the tanks to make sure they had enough oil and supplies and munitions during manoeuvres.

In the middle of the first winter we were part of a vast United Nations operation. In the Tank Corps we would wear full denims, black belts, black holsters and pistols. It rained the entire time and after a few days we were covered in mud. Somehow I managed to contract food poisoning and ended up in a military hospital. For two days I had no idea where I was. Then a nurse came to wake me with some soup. 'How are you feeling now, sir?' she asked, and I said I was much better.

But why was she calling me 'sir'? The following day a sergeant came to take my details. 'Now, sir, what regiment are you in?' he began.

I told him – 6th Royal Tanks.

'Full name, sir,' he requested.

'John Gold,' I said.

As he wrote this down on his clipboard, he half repeated 'Lieutenant Gold.'

'No,' I corrected him, 'Trooper Gold.'

'What?' he exploded. 'Trooper?'

I was moved out of the ward faster than if I'd had leprosy. It was an officers' ward and, because I was carrying a pistol and had no insignia, they had assumed I was one. During the rest of my stay there I was assigned to the job of cutting uniforms off wounded soldiers. They used to reckon on 10 per cent casualties during manoeuvres and most of the poor bastards who were brought in were dispatch riders.

My army career very nearly didn't come to an end after the allotted two years. My dad had written to me saying that he fancied Tulyar in the Derby that year, although the favourite was a horse called Gay Time, ridden by Lester Piggott. We were waiting to start manoeuvres on Lunenberg Heath and a guy from

Birmingham, Chick, who knew I was into racing, suggested we make a book on the Derby because we would be able to listen to the race on the BBC World Service.

So we set up a board and wrote down the runners with the prices from the previous day's paper. Tulyar was at 12-1 but I would offer odds of only 7–2 because of my father's advice, with Gay Time favourite at 6–4. I tried to explain to Chick how you put it down in the book – four pounds to win six against the number of the cloakroom tickets we gave people as tickets for their bets.

The money started cascading in. Not just pounds but Naafi money, German marks and even cigarettes. Word got around and people were coming from other squadrons and regiments with kitbags full of bets.

It was coming in so thick and fast I had no idea where I was. All I knew was that nearly every bet was for Lester Piggott on Gay Time. There was no phone on Lunenberg Heath and no way that I could lay it off.

The race started and men were in clusters all over the Heath listening to Raymond Glendenning on their short-wave radios. It was not a commentary that I will easily forget. 'Here comes Lester Piggott on Gay Time moving up through the field ... and Lester's up with the leaders ... we're in the final furlong, now, and Gay Time has taken the lead.'

My headphones were red-hot. There was no way I was going to be able to pay all the bets. I would be court-martialled and made to stay in the army until I satisfied all my debts, probably for life – that was if I escaped alive from the Heath!

Glendenning's voice moved up a pitch. 'Coming up fast on the outside is Charlie Smirk on Tulyar.' People looked at me as I let out a scream. 'And, at the post, it's Tulyar.' I grabbed hold of Chick and literally threw him up in the air – he was only small.

The great escape!

I have very mixed feelings about my time in Germany – feelings that have never fully been resolved. For the first three months I hated the Germans with such deep-seated venom and resentment that I just refused to go out.

The guys in my unit pointed out that I was hardly punishing the German nation: I was only punishing myself. So I began to go to bars and places where inevitably we mixed with Germans – especially girls – and both the beer and the atmosphere softened any animosity.

I dated German girls. One of them, Gabby, took me back after the pub one evening to her brother's house, where we could make love. On the wall was a picture of their father in full Nazi uniform. I can only report that it didn't inhibit me.

Yet some wounds will never heal. I was selected to play rugby for my regiment against RAF Hohne. It was a very strange day. After the game we had to walk along a path through some woods to reach the RAF mess for a post-match meal. I was seized by a wholly inexplicable sense of nausea and downright fear, which, naturally, I kept to myself.

On the wall of the mess was a notice ordering glider pilots not, under any circumstances, to fly across these woods because there was a dead-air pocket above them. Apparently there had been four crashes, one of them fatal. I wasn't slow in asking. The woods were part of the Bergen-Belsen concentration camp.

That evening, after the game, we went to visit it. The camp had been liberated by British troops less than five years previously. They found thousands of unburied corpses and emaciated and mortally sick inmates. The images that were recorded by photographers there were held up to the world as the greatest of all exhibitions of man's inhumanity.

It still had the stench of death and disease – typhus had spread out of control. It was there that Anne Frank died and it was there that I was happy to turn my back on Germany.

Chapter Four

National service was two years in those days – two *long* years. You couldn't be released from the army into civvy street until you had a final medical confirming you were fit for human life. Mine was to take place in Germany on the Monday we were due to leave for the boat to Harwich and home.

But on the previous Saturday I was asked to play rugby for the 6th Royal Tanks in an important Army Cup match against a regiment in Munster, Westphalia. I declined. I didn't want to sustain any sort of injury and postpone my demob.

But the major in charge prevailed on me and, in front of the medical officer, he promised I would go home – even if I was decapitated. So I played. I had never been injured in two years of rugby in Germany but, almost inevitably, on this occasion I was.

I was playing wing forward and, in a scuffle with the opposition scrum-half, his boot found my knee.

After the match it swelled up like a balloon. I couldn't even limp. The medical officer said I was unfit to travel – but I reminded him of the promise.

So two big chaps, who had been farmers in real life, lifted me up on either side as we marched out of the barracks for the last time. It was a bit like that film *Albert R.N.*, in which Anthony Steel created a dummy with a papier-mâché body and a wire-framed head to cover up for a British prisoner of war who had escaped from a German camp.

Things went fine until we got on the boat – there was no way I could climb down the metal ladder into the section of the ship we had been allocated. I persuaded some petty officer that I suffered so virulently from sea sickness that I had been ordered to stay on deck clinging to the rail or I would make a terrible mess downstairs.

I pretty well crawled on to English soil and I was free. Or nearly. One gentleman in customs was very interested in the stamps on my passport. Why had I never returned home on leave during my entire time in Germany?

I told him the honest truth: 'If I'd come back home, I would never have returned to Germany.'

It didn't endear me to him. Nor did the two thousand cigarettes he found in my kitbag. The limit was two hundred. I explained I had swapped nylons and other duty-free items with guys who had wives and girlfriends.

That cut little ice. He was certain I was up to something. He called a colleague and they started to go through my possessions with a fine-tooth comb, even putting needles through my soap and squeezing out my toothpaste. They ordered me to be strip-searched and smiled with satisfaction when they saw the absurd bandage on my knee. It must be bulging with contraband.

I insisted that a doctor be present as it was unwrapped and pretty soon the massive, repulsive swelling persuaded them that it was a genuine injury.

So I was on my way. They even forgot to fine me for the cigarettes. They were certain I was up to something and they were right. I had carved out the balsa-wood bracketing of my backpack and hidden eight contraband watches in various caches, which I then recovered. A belated apology to all at Her Majesty's Customs and Excise – but I've paid them enough VAT over the years to compensate.

Apart from the knee and the horrors of Belsen, I had escaped from my military service pretty well unscathed. I had seen no combat, but watched the German nation pull themselves together with the generous support of the Allies.

The contrast when I returned to England after two years abroad couldn't have been greater. We were still in a time of austerity – virtually everything was rationed. It was hard to believe we had actually won the war.

Strict government regulation of nearly everything inevitably gave rise to a widespread black market. It seemed to me this was nowhere more flourishing than in my home town.

The big question now facing me and every man who was demobbed was: what am I going to do with the rest of my life?

I went up to London and bunked down at an army buddy's luxurious mouse-infested Soho basement for a few weeks to look for work. My main meal of the day was breakfast, which I had regularly in a café above the Lex Garage round the corner. It was run by an enormously fat guy called Jimmy – his own best customer. It tended to be packed because Jimmy acted on the principle that if you were broke you could pay next time.

For that reason a lot of actors ate there. I was sitting at a table one morning when Jimmy came across and asked, 'Johnny, do you mind if somebody joins you?'

I said that of course I didn't and a dark, good-looking guy with a plate containing an overflowing fry-up sat down opposite me. 'Hello,' he said in a deep voice. 'My name's Richard Burton.'

'I'm Johnny Gold,' I replied. I had never heard of him. He told me he had been an actor in Liverpool but at the end of the war he had had to go into the RAF, where he had served as a navigator.

I told him a bit about my experiences in Germany. He said that he had returned to the stage but it seemed to me that he couldn't have been doing that well, as he appeared to be starving and eagerly wolfed down his breakfast with his fingers, dipping his fried bread into his eggs. However, I sensed he was a passionately ambitious man and I like to think he inspired me to get out there and find a job. (Later, he and his wife, Elizabeth Taylor, offered to back me in a nightclub venture.)

I had a strong feeling that I wanted to travel so I applied to British American Tobacco because I heard they sent you to South America, and that sounded warm and comfortable after Germany. I had three interviews and, somewhat to my amazement, they accepted me. A formal executive pushed a document across a desk. 'Could you just sign that?' he murmured in a throwaway Eton-and-Oxford accent.

Never sign on the dotted line. That was one of the funda-mental rules of life in the army.

'What's the document for?' I enquired.

'In a sense it's for your protection,' he explained. 'It means you don't have to stay in any foreign city for more than four years, but we expect you to do at least two.'

'What cities?' I asked.

'Buenos Aires, Los Angeles, Lima, Karachi – they're all written there.'

'And I select where I want to go,' I said.

'No. We decide, Mr Gold.'

I pushed the document back to him unsigned. After two years in Germany, there was no way I wanted to risk four in Pakistan. Both the man and his superiors were less than pleased with me for wasting their time.

I left, not knowing quite what to do with myself. The easiest thing to do with most decisions is to postpone them, and I was no different from anyone else in this respect. My parents were glad to have me home and my father, Sam, suggested I help out in the SP office.

Officially, people were meant to place bets on credit by phone but they liked to come in and discuss things – just as in betting shops today. And not a few were eager to know what my father, with his actuarial calculations, fancied at the dogs. It was no skin off his nose: he was merely a commission agent and passed the bet on to a licensed bookmaker. Also, it was possible to follow some of the races on the 'blower'.

Of course there was a lot of funny money in those days. And funny people. I used to sit there and learn a lot. I remember one day in particular that was like a scene from a gangster movie. Two men in long overcoats and trilby hats strode in.

My father jumped to his feet. 'Hello, Jack, hello, Martin,' he said. They asked to have a word with him and went into the back room. For no particular reason, Jack came back and said to me, 'You behave yourself, young Gold.'

I had no idea who they were but later learnt that Jack was one of the biggest gangsters in England – Jack Spot.

'Why are there so many crooks in Brighton?' the question used to run. Answer: 'Because the train doesn't go any further.'

There were a lot of people worth avoiding in Brighton at that time but, since most of them liked a bet, they weren't too easy for me to avoid. I seemed to have at the time an unfortunate capacity for attracting friendships with less than savoury people – something that has withered with age.

If not crooks, they were at least very sharp wheeler-dealers. The immediate postwar period was one where the black market held sway. In a paradoxical way the government were partly responsible. They had so much hardware they needed to get rid of that they were giving it away at ridiculous prices. People made fortunes reselling ships and lorries and even submarines to foreign countries.

They were amazing times. Scrap dealers who were used to trading in broken bicycles and bits of guttering or, if they were lucky, iron or copper were now selling second-hand tanks.

There also used to be a lot of antique dealers in Brighton at that time, many of them very well off. The war had caused an upheaval, especially in the South of England, with fatalities in the army or the family business going bust, so dealers would go round the big country houses 'working the knocker'. This meant that they would bang on the door of some stately home, unannounced, and say: 'We just wondered if you had any old antiques or paintings or just bits of rubbish you might want to get rid of.'

Inevitably, people did. Now these guys sounded a bit rough and would pretend to be naïve, but they were really very good judges of antiques. Once inside a house they would look around and very often see an object that they knew was worth a lot of money. Their technique was to earmark something utterly worthless and say to the owner: 'I'll give you a tenner for that' – a lot of money in those days. So the owner would assume they were mugs and accept, but, by the time they came to the piece that the dealer knew he could sell for £500, he would offer the owner a fiver and, more often than not, the offer would be accepted. That was the way they used to work the knocker.

There was a barrow-boy fraternity in Brighton – the sort of people who always managed to produce black-market goods such as nylons. So, with them and the antique boys and the people who lived by betting, there was an array of characters in the town who would have given the novelist Damon Runyon plenty of new material.

These characters had names like Swanker, Bladder, the Head and Pudding. I remember, on one occasion, a police officer coming up to Pudding, who was nursing a Perrier at the bar at about a quarter to four, long after hours for the consumption of alcohol.

'What are you drinking?' he demanded.

'That's very kind of you,' Pudding replied. 'I'll have a gin and tonic.'

They were the real racecourse characters. In another league was Frankie Fraser, whom I knew from the betting shop and who seemed to take a liking to me and kept insisting: 'Come and have a drink.' At first I did, but then I was warned he was a 'psycho' and started giving him a wide berth. I think he must have been at the height of his hit-man powers around then.

Fortunately, he started to go out with the daughter of Gus the Presser (so called because he pressed clothes in a little dry-cleaning shop). Gus was understandably perturbed about this and, knowing I had an 'in' to Frankie, asked me if I could tell him to terminate the relationship.

'You want me to tell Frankie to stop taking out your daughter?' I repeated incredulously. 'Are you mad?'

'No,' said Gus, dismayed.

'Well *he* certainly is,' I told him. 'He'd cut me up into little pieces.'

I wasn't far wrong. Some years later Frankie had a fight with a man called Eric Mason in the Astor Club. Mason warned him he was going to tell the Kray twins – a fatal error. Frankie bundled him into the back of his car, took him out on a piece of waste ground, then chopped him up with an axe and left his remains in a bag.

Frankie was to spend forty of the next fifty years in jail but in 2000 he was the only one from the 'old gang' called to the bedside of the dying Reggie Kray and now has a website, appropriately called 'Mad Frankie', with details of the Kray and Richardson gangs and even a tour of criminal east London. Who says crime doesn't pay – although forty years inside is quite a price.

After I had been in the SP office a few months and learnt the system, my father had to go to London on business and left me in charge of the office. There was only one small meeting on at Bath so we hardly expected to be very busy. However, the phone rang and somebody said he'd like £25 each way on a horse called Francascal. Before I took it, I called a bookmaker to lay it off but he said, 'I'm full up.' I called every bookmaker we knew. None of them would take it. I was going out of my mind.

Francascal romped home at 16–1, leaving me to explain to my
father why we were out £500 on the race. I sensed my SP career
coming to an abrupt halt.

But it was a scam. Not only had the guys who had arranged it
cut all the lines to the course so no news of the betting could get
back but they had also switched horses. Nobody got paid out.
The culprits were arrested and spent some time inside.

A friend of mine, knowing I was looking for a job, invited me
up to London to meet Jack Delal who, at the time, was one of
the wealthiest men in England and still is. He was an imposing
man, short but with an outsize personality. He asked me if I
would like to become his south coast 'spotter', which meant
driving round the south coast to see if there was anything for
sale that he could turn around for a profit. I would get a good
commission on any deal.

I agreed. I had a Hillman Minx and drove between Hastings
and Bexhill and Brighton and Worthing and Southampton
looking for something appropriate. I did it for three months and
never spotted a suitable house.

It was probably just as well. I've sometimes thought since then
that, if I'd made a lot of money in that job, I would never have
had such a great time in the life I love.

I have to confess to a certain addiction to cinema at the time. I
didn't have the looks of a Roger Moore to be in the Rank charm
school or anything, but friends suggested I didn't look bad at the
other end of a camera. So, without a great deal of modesty, I went
along to London Films because they were looking for extras.

And I was hired. The name of the film was *Mr Denning Drives
North* but it was shot under some title like *Teddy Bear* or *Little
Bear*. My big moment of stardom was to stand and watch a body
being washed up on a beach. I keep telling the children to look
out for it on late-night TV.

Sam Wanamaker was in the movie and was a very

approachable man. He had fought in the war but had found postwar Hollywood an uncomfortable place to be because of his leftist political associations and the McCarthy witch-hunt, so he started a new life in Britain – greatly to our benefit, because without him there would be no Shakespeare Globe Theatre.

I told him how Edward G Robinson nearly gave us a home as a family. Sam said that Robinson had been hauled up before the House Un-American Activities Committee because of his association with communist front organisations. He was completely exonerated, but the mud stuck.

How ironic that Wanamaker, who fought for his country, and Robinson, who at 47 was too old to do so but was renowned for his activity in patriotic causes, should have been dragged so low.

I got another job in a short film called *Find the Duchess*, which was being made to promote the Glyndebourne Opera in Sussex. It wasn't far from Brighton and we used to be bussed there to arrive at six in the morning. As you got out of the bus in the still, summer dawn you could hear the opera stars going up and down the scales as they exercised their voices first thing in the morning. It really was electrifying.

There was a sequence in which the Royal Philharmonic relaxed and played croquet in the gracious grounds. They were slightly short of members so the assistant director shoved me in.

'Who are you?' demanded the orchestra leader.

'Oh, I'm the new first oboe,' I replied. I'm glad I didn't have to stand in on the night.

However, I was used as a stand-in for Cesto Bruscantini, the most famous tenor of the day, on the main stage where the BBC were preparing to film the evening performance. I was placed in the middle of the stage with lots of technicians and people around getting the camera angles and the lighting right.

A man dressed in a brown boiler suit, slightly short in the leg and revealing his multicoloured socks, minced across the stage towards me. It was Anthony Asquith, the director.

'Who are you, then?' he demanded in a clipped voice.

'I'm standing in for Don Giovanni,' I replied.

'Wrong opera, pet.' He smiled as he ruffled my hair. 'We're doing *Figaro*.'

And he minced off again, much to the amusement of all in the auditorium.

Glyndebourne was a highly sexed place and both Asquith and the designer, Oliver Messell, who had a broken collarbone at the time, made several advances towards my young body. I became nimble in avoiding them and still managed to hold on to my job, and actually enjoyed a wardrobe relationship with a very pretty soprano from the chorus called Kitty.

My final thespian performance was in a commercial with the nightclub owner Helen Cordet, known at the time to be a 'very good friend' of Prince Philip. I merely had to pass her table in a club and light her cigarette.

It took me 26 takes. After that I found it more agreeable to have friends who were actors than to attempt to be one.

Chapter Five

During the early fifties in Brighton, I helped my father in the SP office and managed to get out of the office by working for a dog bookmaker called Harry Saffron. I was 21 and I used to drive him in his car, a beautiful Jaguar, to White City and Harringay and Wembley in London. At the track my job was to be 'on the bag' – people placed their bets, you put the money in the bag and, after the race, paid it out to the winners.

Harry made an absolute fortune. There was so much cash around at the time– a flourishing black market, as I've said – and people coming out of the services with large sums of back pay. For a bookmaker at the dogs it was a licence to print money.

Harry was a smooth bachelor and after a dog meeting he loved to go out on the town. Our first port of call was always the Nightingale in Berkeley Square (where Mortons now is). Then it was on to Winstons or the Eve or the Astor or Churchills. These were real nightclubs, which served drinks and dinner and put on big cabaret shows. The club owners were larger-than-life characters: Harry Meadows, Bertie Green and Bruce Brace. They wore carnations, had big cigars and bigger bellies and were just outrageous.

Harry always used to invite me to have dinner with him. The nightspots were flowing with cash and girls. Harry had no difficulty finding a date for the night and there were sometimes two or three girls in the Jag when we drove back to his penthouse in Hove in the early hours of the morning.

It was my first contact with nightlife. I found it exciting and I was greatly drawn to it. Shades of things to come.

At the same time I became friendly with a man who moved to Brighton called Michael Black. He said that he owned a chain of sweetshops and garages throughout England. He opened a coffee shop – very trendy those days – on the seafront at Brighton and put his attractive blonde 'wife', Susan, in to run it, as he was often away in London on business.

He threw a surprise 21st-birthday party for me. I remember it well because my family never really believed very much in birthdays. I had just planned to go out for a couple of drinks with a friend of mine called Raymond Williams (we're still friends 45 years later). He suggested we should pop by Michael's coffee bar to see if he was in town and they said, 'Sure, he's downstairs.' Curiously it was very dark in the basement. Then the lights went on and there was Michael with all my friends. He'd arranged the whole thing – it was a very wild and happening night.

A few months later I was walking along the seafront and bumped into Paddy the Thief – so called because he was a professional thief. In the course of our conversation he asked me, 'How's your friend, Michael?'

I said that I hadn't seen him for some time. I thought he was in bed in London with gout.

'Gout!' Paddy repeated derisively. 'He's as fit as a fiddle. He has to be – he's the best bloody cat burglar in Britain. He can shoot up a twenty-foot wall like nobody you've ever seen in your life.'

This was as big a surprise as my birthday party. I couldn't really believe it and I certainly never mentioned it to Michael. But one evening he and I were walking down an alleyway in Brighton and some tramp jumped out of the shadows and demanded money from us. He was a wisp of a man and very drunk. But Michael suddenly went mad and grabbed him by the throat. For a moment I thought he was going to kill him. As I pulled him off, I said, 'Michael, if you were to blow on this guy he would fall over.'

I could now see there was a dark and dangerous side to Michael. And I later discovered he lived a complete lie. Susan wasn't his wife, she was a girlfriend, in fact a nightclub hostess from Churchills in Bond Street.

We saw less of each other until some years later, after I had moved to London. I was going out with a girl called Cynthia Black (no relation to Michael), whose model agency had entered her for the Miss Great Britain competition, which she won under the name Sonya Hamilton. She was absolutely stunning and one of the first big loves in my life. But she thought we should get married and I thought I wasn't ready – I'd yet to find my true vocation. So, reluctantly, I ended our relationship.

Cynthia actually lived in Brighton and one morning Michael telephoned me and said, 'I'm so upset you two've broken up. You were perfect for each other. Do you mind if I take Cynthia out and try and patch things up?'

I told him, 'Michael, by all means take her out. But don't think you'll get us together again. You won't.'

Then one morning – it can't have been more than six weeks later – he came to see me. He seemed uncomfortable. 'I didn't want you to hear it from anybody else but I'm going on holiday to Majorca and I'm taking Cynthia with me.'

I said, 'Fine by me,' but, in truth, I was a bit choked because he was meant to be a friend.

Then he blurted out, 'We're going to get married.'

I heard myself saying 'Congratulations'. What else could I say?

I heard nothing more from either of them for three months until one morning the phone rang at two o'clock. It was Cynthia.

'Are you alone?' she asked. I said I was and she said she was coming over.

It had been raining heavily and she was soaking as she sat on my sofa – but still as beautiful as ever.

'You've got to tell me about Michael,' she demanded.

I played dumb. 'What do you mean?'

'I've found his gun,' she said.

'It would have been more sensible if you'd asked me this question before you rushed off and married him. All I can say is that I've heard rumours that he could possibly be involved in some kind of villainy. It's only hearsay.'

That was it. She left him. And he completely went to pieces. He was caught on the roof of a house in Hampstead, trying to break in, and was sent to jail. In prison he had a heart attack – although he was only 33. When he was released, he went back to his house in Seymour Place in London, caught pneumonia, had another heart attack and died. I spoke to Cynthia a couple of times on the phone, but two years later she committed suicide.

Michael had introduced me to a friend of his called Alan Brown, a very tall, elegant man who had a Norwegian wife called Winky. By night Alan ran his club, the Bucket of Blood, on the seafront at Brighton, and by day he was a scrap dealer. Not just any scrap dealer. There was a huge aircraft called the Brabazon at the time, which turned out to be a complete disaster. And they needed an even bigger crane to get it in and out of the hangar. Alan bought this from the British government for £2,000 and sold it to the Belgian government for £25,000.

But he also had a criminal record.

I'll always remember one thing he did for me, earlier in our friendship. I had been shopping with Michael Black at Simpsons in Piccadilly (now sadly closed down). Michael was a real Raffles, beautifully dressed, looked immaculate all the time. He was buying clothes as if there was no tomorrow.

My eye fell on this smart tweed coat and I tried it on. Wonderful! In fact it cost £50 and I had about £90 to my name at that time and less than £10 in my pocket. Michael said I had to have it, lent me the £50, which I paid him back the following day, and I walked out of the store feeling like a million dollars.

I wore it to the Churchills' staff party the following Sunday night but not home again, because somebody stole it from the cloakroom. I was choked, even more so since this was a private party given by the hostesses and not covered by the club's insurance. I never saw the coat again.

The following night Alan Brown gave a Christmas party. I was still pretty pissed off about the stolen coat, which he knew about. Alan and Winky came over to where I was sitting and he said, 'Come and dance with Winky.' As I got up he pressed something into my palm with the words 'Happy Christmas'.

It was a cheque for £150. I gave it back to him straightaway, saying, 'I can't accept this.'

He took me to one side. 'Listen, you graft your little bollocks off day and night to earn nothing, just because you're straight. Us thieves get money very easily. It comes and it goes. If you think you're going to give this back, I'll break your fucking neck. Now go and dance with Winky.'

That was Alan.

One morning he got a visit from a Brighton police sergeant, who told him they were going to arrest him for a robbery that had taken place in Eastbourne at the weekend. 'We know your background – we're going to do you for it.'

The sergeant did offer him a way out – if he was prepared to pay him two thousand pounds.

Alan was shocked. He knew that, if he paid, the guy would be back for more money. So he took the bull by the horns and went with his lawyer to Scotland Yard and told them what had happened.

This initiated a wholesale investigation into the Brighton police. In this postwar world of fast deals and fast money they were determined not to be left out. The corruption went up as far as the chief constable.

Alan Brown, as chief witness for the Crown, was assured the case would be held in camera.

The police love giving people criminal names like 'the Weasel' or 'the Nark' just to make them sound more guilty in the eyes of the public. Brighton police lost no time in dubbing Alan 'the Toff' and making sure Alan's record was prominently revealed in the papers, local and national.

So much for 'in camera'. The case became front-page news: the Toff versus the Brighton police. On the night before the trial I had a call from Alan. He was really depressed. I was living in London by then and went over to his mews house by Marble Arch. We sat having a Scotch and watched the evening news, which featured pictures of him and details of the pending trial.

Emboldened by a few drinks, he got up and said, 'Well, fuck it. If they want to call me the Toff, they'll *get* the Toff.'

He opened this huge wardrobe, which stretched the length of his room, containing dozens of suits, and asked me, 'Which one shall I wear tomorrow?' He settled for a well-cut pinstripe, a two-tone shirt with a stiff white collar, a striped silk tie and dark-grey fedora – the whole thing.

To cut a long story sideways, the police were all found guilty. But Alan was ruined as well. With his record paraded in public he could no longer do business with foreign governments, let alone continue to get the huge loans from the banks to finance his deals. He ended up with a little hotel in Jersey. That was the last I ever heard of him.

I hasten to point out that not all my friends were criminals, but in the era of the 'gentleman criminal' it was hard to tell who was and who wasn't. The temptations were there at that time and they were great.

But not for me. I had needed to get away from Brighton and find an honest job. At first I followed my father into the fashion industry in the East End of London. For the princely sum of twelve pounds a week I would put the coats on a metal stand with a cardboard cutout on it, chalk in the points where the three buttonholes should go and then chuck them to the machinists.

It was the most soul-destroying time of my life. I thought I was going to become a basket case. Until, one day, I saw the manager on the phone reading from a piece of paper in front of him. I knew exactly what he was doing and it wasn't ordering buttons. I went up to him.

'Do you want to have a bet?' he asked, indicating the piece of paper. 'I'm phoning all these bets away for the girls on the machines.'

'I think I can save you a lot of time,' I said.

He was only too pleased to hand over the job to me and through my father's office I could do it very quickly. The bets from the staff were small – two bob each way, five shillings to win, that sort of thing – but it meant I made a bit of commission every day and that certainly helped.

Nevertheless, I couldn't put up with the job for more than three months and eventually resigned. By luck, shortly after that I was sitting beside a man at dinner who asked me, 'What do you do for a living?'

So I told him, 'I've got my old job back.'

'What's that?' he asked.

'Looking for a job,' I replied sardonically.

He was in the rag trade, too, and needed an allocations clerk. I had no idea what this was, so he explained: 'Suppose you're a buyer and you like Style Number One and you want two sizes in red and three in blue and four in white – I would call those out as your order and you would get them all together.'

It seemed easy enough but he had a word of warning: 'The fellow who's in charge is a real arsehole and everybody's terrified of him.'

I took the job but his final words proved completely correct.

This man was a gorilla who kept yelling and throwing his weight about and complaining that everything I did was wrong. I had faced this situation before in the barrack room with Johnny Paynter and resolved on my third day as an allocations clerk to do something about it. He started rubbishing me first thing in the morning and I just went up to him and said, very quietly, 'Can we talk?'

He was already taken aback. I continued: 'Listen, if you don't like me why don't you sort it out with me outside, down in the dispatch area? Then we'll both be happy. We can knock lumps out of each other. If that will make you happy, it will make me happy. Otherwise, get off my back and we'll all be friends.'

I held my breath for a bit – this was the sort of guy who swung from rafters – but, like all bullies, he capitulated and, from then on, our relationship was perfectly workable.

I rose to the giddy heights of becoming personal assistant to Harold Lee, who had engaged me. We had showrooms in Margaret Street with a warehouse down in the City, just off Old Street. One day Harold asked me to escort two very serious female buyers down to the warehouse.

'Be on your best behaviour,' he advised me. 'They are very genteel ladies.'

He had no need to do that. I drove them very carefully down to Old Street and, like a chauffeur, jumped out of the car to open their door.

There was a really filthy lorry on the other side of the road, full of scrap. Its door opened and a dishevelled, dirt-encrusted man jumped down and came towards me.

'It's Johnny Gold,' he called out. 'It's fuckin' Johnny Gold.'

He hugged me and bounced me up and down. The two women buyers looked on in some amazement. It was Johnny Paynter, my old mate from the army. I was so thrilled to see him that I completely forgot about my two passengers whose expressions, by now, had changed from amazement to horror. But they were very understanding when I explained it all later.

Another incident I recall from that time was when I was heading for home down Jermyn Street and bumped into a couple of guys I knew, Monty Marks and Brian Morris. They were about to go into a club, the Crazy Elephant, and they insisted I join them. I literally had no money on me – and very little under the mattress – so I protested that I was broke. But they dragged me down into the club, where Brian bought a round of Scotches.

Then they went off to look for a girl in another room and I was left finishing my drink on my own. Next thing I knew a voice boomed in my ear: 'Hey kid, is anybody sitting here?'

The voice was familiar and, when I looked up, so was the face. It was John Wayne. He was with another couple – a man and a woman – and announced: 'I'm sitting next to you kid.'

My first thought, I promise, was: Don't tell me he's queer. I'd had enough of that at Glyndebourne. But he wasn't. What he was was extremely drunk.

'How come you ain't with a chick?' he demanded.

'I don't know. Just one of those things, I suppose,' I replied.

'I've had more chicks than went down with the *Titanic*,' he announced.

Just then a pretty girl walked by. She stopped in amazement when she saw John Wayne – by far the number-one box-office star in the world at the time.

'Are you by yourself?' he demanded.

'Yes,' she replied eagerly, thinking she was going to be with John Wayne.

'Well, come on over,' he said. 'You're with the kid.'

I watched her face fall as she sat down. The drinks began to flow and Monty and Brian, seeing who I was now with, returned and pulled up chairs at the table.

Wayne pointed at Monty. 'See his nose – busted.' Then at Brian. 'See his nose – busted.' He touched his own nose. 'See my nose . . .'

'Busted,' I said.

'Exactly,' said the very drunk Wayne, 'and I'm going to bust your nose, kid.'

He waved a fist in front of me that was twice as large as both of mine put together.

I found myself saying, 'Stand up and say that.'

He looked at me and stood up and I followed suit, reluctantly. He was a huge man, towering over me by more than a foot.

'I'm packing a gun, kid,' he warned.

I patted my jacket. 'Oh, God, I've left mine in my other suit.'

Wayne roared with laughter, and brought his hand down on my shoulder, half breaking it. 'You're all right, kid. Sit down.'

I felt I had just been in a John Wayne movie and told him so.

'You just play yourself,' I said naïvely.

'I'll bust your nose, kid,' he growled.

I told him how he had once had me in hysterics. During my national service in Germany I had seen a dubbed version of *Red River*. 'At the end of the film you're coming through the cattle to kill Montgomery Clift. John Ireland shoots you and you shoot him but you keep going. The music comes to a crescendo and Montgomery Clift turns to you and the two of you are face to face and, in the German version, you say, "Achtung" in this high-pitched voice. I just fell off my seat, laughing.'

Wayne, thankfully, joined in the general laughter round the table and then asked me, 'Do you know what I was really saying, kid?'

I shook my head.

'Burn 'em,'

I still didn't know.

'Burn 'em,' he repeated, rising to his feet. 'Burn the leather, get your gun out of your holster.'

He proceeded to re-enact the whole of the last five minutes of *Red River* for my benefit – and the rest of the table.

When it was time to go he made me promise to write to Paul

Newman – 'Tell him you had a great time with the Duke' – and said that I should visit him on the set of a film he was making.

I duly promised. But, fool that I was, I never went, especially as his co-stars were Gina Lollobrigida and Claudia Cardinale. Some years later his two sons, Michael (a producer) and Patrick (an actor), came to the club. I told them the story of my night with their dad. I said, 'He won't remember, but please give him my best wishes. Tell him I didn't write to Paul Newman, but I did tell Paul when he came to the club that the Duke was a good guy and that I'd had a great night with him, just as your dad requested.' A few days later, Michael and Patrick returned and said, 'Dad remembers the night and wants you to come and have lunch on the set of *Brannigan.*' I was thrilled, but unfortunately the Duke got pneumonia and shooting was stopped for a few weeks. After that, schedules were so tight that lunch was cancelled. However, his sons brought me a belt buckle, on the back of which was inscribed: 'To Johnny, from your pal, the Duke.' I still treasure it today.

Chapter Six

I had moved to London shortly before my 23rd birthday. While I was moving around jobs in the clothing trade, I found a flat – all right, a room – in Sussex Gardens, just north of Hyde Park. It was in the basement of a place called Stephen's Court and cost me £4 a week which didn't leave me with a lot of loose change from my £12-a-week salary, reduced to about £8 after tax and other deductions.

When I had answered an advertisement in the *Evening Standard* for a room with bath, I had not expected the bath to be actually *in* the room. But it was. It dominated it. You placed a prudish wooden lid on top of it when it was not in use, rather as the Victorians covered up the legs of their grand pianos.

A friend lent me an old black-and-white television with an indoor aerial, which had a wonderfully distorted picture (I could never recognise anybody on TV) but very good sound.

A girl I knew rang me one day and asked me what I was doing. 'I'm in the bath, watching television,' I told her.

The next time we met she was with a friend, who said to me, 'I hear you live in some luxury.'

'Really?' I enquired.

'Yes,' he said, 'you have a television in the bathroom.'

I obligingly agreed – although it was, in fact, a bath in the television room.

To my increasing satisfaction, about 85 per cent of the other tenants of Stephen's Court were single girls. There were dancers, models, nightclub hostesses, show girls and three hookers. I adored one of the hookers, Trudy. She used to have me in hysterics, describing the antics of her clients. She was on the books of two embassies and really something special. Knowing that I wasn't that flush, she used to take me out when she wasn't working and I was worried that people thought I was a pimp. Trudy ended up marrying a Texan multimillionaire. I still get a card from them every Christmas.

One evening I met an attractive girl in the lift and we fell into conversation. She asked me what I did and I, with the usual deprecation, said my job tended to be looking for other jobs. I asked her what she did and she said she was a singer. I would have recognised her from my television if the picture had been better.

Marion Ryan started out as a singer with Edmundo Ross and made her name on a TV show called *Spot The Tune* with Jackie Ray. It was a forerunner of *Name That Tune*, only she would sing all the snippets of a song. It made her famous – at least in houses with clear television pictures.

We went on to become good friends. She had a large apartment at the top of the block. I think nearly all television was live in those days and I would go up to her flat and watch her on TV shows such as *Off the Record* and *Jack Jackson's Record Round-Up*.

Afterwards she would take me to the opening of various restaurants and the Talk of the Town, where she became an established favourite with the Ray Ellington Quartet (famous from *The Goon Show*).

Marion had twin sons who went on to have careers as pop singers. I can remember picking them up for her from Liverpool Street Station when they were in short trousers. Paul and Barry's biggest hit, 'Eloise', was famous for being one of the longest songs in the charts – it lasted more than five minutes. Marion was proud of them: it reached number two, three places higher than her most-remembered hit, 'Love Me Forever'.

Thanks to the education, if that's the right word, from Harry Saffron, I already had a reasonably sophisticated knowledge of London nightlife and continued to enjoy it with him from time to time. However, on my own, with about £4 disposable income, I tended not to live on champagne.

But the clubs did come in useful to the lowly paid. In those days the licensing laws were such that you were not allowed to have a drink without having anything to eat. So Mark Rudolph, a similarly paid friend, and I would pop along to the Astor, where we knew quite a lot of people, and feast on their sandwiches. Later, they changed the law, saying you had to have *hot* food, which really pissed me off because there went supper.

It was on such a sandwich night that Mark nudged me and pointed out Ella Fitzgerald with Oscar Peterson. She caught my eye as I was staring at her and gave me a smile. I turned back to talk to Mark but, without warning, I was pulled up out of my chair by the collar.

'Come and dance with Ella,' Miss Fitzgerald commanded, and I was in no position to turn her down.

She was an enormous star and an enormous woman, but light on her feet. I told her she danced much better than I did and she replied, 'Honey, if you think I can move now, you should see what I'm like in bed.'

This set off a warning light in my brain, which proved only too accurate when, during a slow number, she had me in this huge bear hug – we must have looked like something out of a Disney cartoon – and whispered, 'Honey, you're coming back to the Dorchester with me.'

'Yeah, sure,' I croaked and, at the first opportunity, escorted her back to Oscar Peterson.

I returned to Mark and whispered, 'Listen, I'm going to

pretend to go to the loo but in fact I'm going to shoot up those stairs as fast as I can. Meet me at the top in two minutes.'

He did so, unquestioningly. As he reached the top, I could hear Ella – who was sitting close to the bottom of the stairs – call up, 'Johnny, baby, where are you going?'

The next morning I was awakened by a call from Marion. She sounded angry.

'What the hell have you been up to? Who was that big, fat, black woman you were dancing with last night?'

I rubbed my eyes. 'You're not going to believe this, but it was...'

'Ella Fitzgerald.' She finished my sentence for me. '*I* know that – but think of all the people who don't!'

There was a curious sequel to that incident. One night Mark and I were just about to leave the Astor Club when he said to me, 'Don't look now, but Marion's just walked in with Harold Davidson and what looks like Count Basie.'

'Can we sneak away?' I asked.

He shook his head. 'No. You've been spotted.'

So I went over to their table and, as casually as I could, said: 'Hi, Marion, hi, Harold.'

She gave me an icy stare and he gave me an even icier one since he suspected I was seeing her, as well. (It was at a time before he even managed her; later they got married.) But that night, because of their guests, Harold was forced to be polite.

'Johnny, this is Bill Basie and his wife and Buddy Greco and his wife.'

I was pretty much in awe of meeting two of my heroes at once and was certainly a bit disorientated when suddenly Buddy Greco's wife jumped up and said, 'Let's dance.'

I glanced across at the table where her husband was sitting. He didn't seem to be too thrilled.

'I don't think your husband likes us dancing this close,' I stuttered.

'Oh, fuck him,' she said, pointing to her right eye. 'Look at this, that bastard did it to me.'

There was a slight mark below her eyebrow. I told her, 'Listen, if you want to make your husband angry, please leave me out of this.'

When I escorted her back to the table he was still looking daggers at me but said nothing. Marion was pissed off with me and Harold didn't look too happy, either.

For the second time that year, I made a hasty exit from the Astor Club.

Of course, in years to come, all of them would come to Tramp. Harold and Marion would sometimes bring Frank Sinatra, whom Harold represented in Europe.

Poor Marion – she died just a couple of years ago. She was quite something. Her vivacious charm was recorded on celluloid in the film she made with Tommy Steele, Shane Fenton and Russ Conway, *It's All Happening*.

Despite my lowly status by day, I met quite a lot of characters at Bertie Green's Astor Club – it wouldn't take a lot of sessions with the psychiatrist to discover what finally made a club my career.

I remember in particular Tommy Yeardye, who was known as Mr Muscle – he was tall and very handsome. He was going out with Diana Dors (née Fluck) at the time. Diana was never very proud of the movies she was making – they had titles such as *Lady Jodi Rides Again* and *Is Your Honeymoon Really Necessary?* and *The Wild and the Wicked* – but showed the world she could really act in *Yield to the Night*, when she played a woman in a condemned cell.

I thought she was great and told her so. She said how hard it had been to change the public perception of her, although with her spilling blonde hair and great boobs I wondered how hard she had tried. Tommy was a man with a good eye for what was fashionable. He went into partnership with Vidal Sassoon and, later, with his daughter, Tamara, ran Jimmy Choo, which made popular – as a girl in Tramp once described them – 'follow me, fuck me' shoes.

As I've said, my father was friendly with the Crazy Gang – Bud Flanagan, Chesney Allen, Jimmy Nervo and Monsieur Eddie Gray – and from time to time I would bump into them on the club scene. They played the Victoria Palace for many years and Eddie Gray offered me a couple of tickets for their new show. I was going out with Cynthia at the time and our seats were in the front row of the theatre, where we sat holding hands.

At the start of the evening Bud, Chesney, Jimmy and Eddie all came on stage individually to huge applause. Then they all linked hands and, looking down at Cynthia and me, went in unison, 'Ahhhh.' As Wilfred Pickles used to say – was my face red?

There was more to come. They were doing a Robin Hood sketch later in the show with Eddie Gray up in the box and Bud Flanagan down on the stage as the Sheriff of Nottingham. He shouted out, 'Where's Maid Marion?' and Eddie shouted back, 'Who's made Marion?'

'Give us a chance,' said Bud, 'we've only been open for two weeks.'

Then Eddie came back: 'Well you'd better watch it – Johnny Gold's in the audience tonight.'

It was shortly after that evening that the strangest thing happened to me, which I have never been able to explain – even to myself.

I had been working for Harold Lee in the fashion business. I was doing sales and I knew the buyers and many of the people in the industry. We used to have what were known as 'outdoor workers' to whom we passed on our orders, and these tailors would make up the coats and dresses and whatever.

Harold, unfortunately, went broke, so I decided to set up on my own and I did a deal with one of these outdoor workers, Joe, that he would make all the coats for me and I would use his facilities – offices, factory, phones and so forth – and, in return, would give him 20 per cent of the profits of my business. It worked out very well and I started making some real money.

There was a secretary in Joe's office called Mary. One day she brought a frail little woman in her late sixties into my office and introduced her to me: 'This is Mrs Sharrock and she needs to talk to you.'

I sized her up; she certainly didn't look like a conventional buyer. I offered her a chair and asked, 'What can I do for you?'

She answered with a question. 'Do you believe in spiritualism?'

As it happened, I did. I had had an experience with some boys when I was younger. My friend, Maurice Hyams, actually had parents who were spiritualists. One night he held a séance for Raymond Williams (both are still friends) and me and two others with a ouija board. We used it to locate a girl who had died and whom we had all known. Somebody asked her a rude question. Immediately a book flew off the mantelpiece and crashed into the door. It had scared the wits out of me. We turned the lights on and there was no string or wire or anything. It certainly wasn't a trick.

I told Mrs Sharrock this. She shook her head. 'That's not what I do. I have so many messages for you.' She mentioned some name I had never heard of and my reaction was that she was wasting my time. But then she said, 'Who's Sam?'

I was taken aback. 'My father,' I told her. Then I realised this was hardly classified information.

'And Sarah?'

'My mother.' I was less than impressed. She reeled off some other names but they meant nothing to me. As she left, she gave me a card and told me to come and visit her if I needed to.

That weekend I went home to Brighton and happened to mention to my father over supper my experience with Mrs Sharrock. 'She kept mentioning the name "Susan",' I told him.

'That was the name of my younger sister,' he replied. 'She was in a fire and got burnt to death when she was only fourteen.'

Then I mentioned two foreign-sounding names that came up. It transpired they were the Russian names of my grandparents – I had only ever known them as Grandma and Grandpa.

Three weeks later my father died of a heart attack. I was shattered. He was the best thing in my life. We were so close. He was the only person in the world I could tell absolutely everything to and I loved him dearly. I had been blessed with wonderful parents.

I temporarily moved back to Brighton to be with my mother, who was alone. My business was going better than ever but I wasn't happy. My father's death affected me more than I could have anticipated. With hindsight, I think it was because he hadn't lived to see me do anything with my life or settle down or, even, provide him with grandchildren.

Two weeks later Mrs Sharrock arrived at the office again. 'I was sorry to hear about your father,' she said, 'but I've come here to tell you he's been in touch with me.' She looked at me. 'You're standing just the way he stands.'

I realised that I was, one hand in my pocket and one fingering my chin. She could never have seen him – but she could have guessed.

'I don't understand it,' she continued, 'but he kept showing me two small objects. At first I thought they were cufflinks, but then they seemed more like coins. But small coins. Your father said to me, "You tell him about the coins, then he'll believe you."'

This was serious. My great-grandfather, who was a trader, had two South African half-sovereigns which had been passed down the male line, eventually from my father to me. I took them out of my pocket and showed them to her. (Many years later they fell out of my pocket on a plane and my son Nicky, bless him, tracked down a similar pair and gave them to me for my fiftieth birthday.)

My mind sort of froze and I cannot remember all the other

things she told me, but she integrated correct facts about our family that she couldn't have known with reassurances that my father was 'all right'.

This experience coincided with the worst time of my life. My days became more exhausting. I left Brighton before five in the morning to get to the East End factory by six. I'd work there until about twelve and then drive back to Brighton to the SP office and work there until the end of racing. After that I would drive back to the factory for a couple of hours and then back home to Brighton where I would collapse in a heap. I did this for a year without a break and I finally realised it was going to kill me. I was going to have to give something up.

Eventually I confessed to Mary: 'I need to see Mrs Sharrock.'

Mary smiled. 'She'll be thrilled.'

She lived in a little council flat in the East End of London. By way of what I thought to be small talk I asked her how she had become a medium. She told me that her daughter had been killed in an accident. She was run over when she was just a little girl. Mrs Sharrock had gone to all sorts of mediums to try to get in touch with her but they all proved to be phoneys.

Then, out of the blue, she was contacted by what she described as 'this scout' who led her into the other world. And there she realised that she, herself, had powers and was able to contact her daughter on her own.

'I have the silver thread...' she began to explain.

But I knew the expression. As a boy, Maurice Hyams had taken me to a spiritualist meeting with his parents. The medium had unwaveringly picked on me – 'I must talk to that young man.'

I thought: Holy shit!

But he said that he had strong messages for me and they were only good things. And he was accurate, as accurate as Mrs Sharrock (I never did learn her first name). And that was where I learnt about the 'silver thread' – people who are slightly psychic, who can pick up things. Half of me thinks it's bullshit;

the other half thinks there's something in it. However, I don't want to get hooked.

But, when you're desperate, cool logic isn't at the top of your emotions. I desperately needed to know what to do with the rest of my life.

I remember we sat opposite each other in hard-back chairs. Mrs S, who must have been seventy then and frailer than before, put her hands together, locking her fingers.

She held them up before me. 'Place your hands on my wrists and pull them apart,' she instructed me. 'It will show you the strength of the bond between you and your father.'

I tried so hard I lifted her out of her chair. But I couldn't make her fingers budge.

'You see,' she said, 'the bond between you and your father cannot be broken.'

Then she told me my father wanted me to give up the fashion business. I should go home to Brighton and run my father's business and be with my mother. Later, something else would come along.

I tried to weigh up the pros and cons as I walked down the iron staircase from her flat. She was an honest woman, I knew that. I had begged her to take money for her time but she refused, saying she would burn it. So I had brought chocolates and flowers.

She rang me some weeks later, saying she had more messages from my father and he was desperate to get in touch with me. But I had thought the matter through and told her, 'With all due respect, I loved my father more than anything. But I think he, more than anybody, would understand that if I depend on the spiritual world for my decisions it would control me. He wouldn't want that.'

Mrs Sharrock did not give up lightly. 'Imagine if he had been round the world on a trip and he came home. Would you slam the door in his face?'

'Of course not,' I said.

'That's exactly what you are doing,' she replied.

I was sure her motives were entirely pure and for what she saw to be my benefit, but I was adamant. 'You may feel that way, but I really don't want to get involved again. I'm sorry.'

That was the last occasion on which we spoke. I never saw her again and she died many years ago.

Maybe my decision was wiser than I realised. Two brothers whom I knew were in business together and they consulted another medium frequently. One day they were having a session with him and the door of the room locked itself from the inside. The medium told them that they must not unlock the door until it opened itself. They sat there for five hours until the door did, indeed, unlock itself and in that time they had hammered out a business plan with the help of the medium.

Subsequently, they went bust.

But I shall always be grateful to Mrs Sharrock. She guided me out of the worst period of my life and put me on the first stepping stone towards what was about to become the best.

Chapter Seven

So I remained in Brighton and ran my father's – well, it was now my – SP business. In those days it was nearly always telephone betting; betting shops, as such, had barely begun to surface.

We were, in effect, commission agents. We gave credit to our clients, who had accounts with us, and passed on their bets to big bookmakers. In return we earned a small commission – up to 5 per cent – with no loss to the client, rather in the manner travel companies get commission for selling airline tickets.

Local people came to us because we were convenient and gave generous credit. Some settled weekly; others settled very weakly. But I think the main reason we were quite popular and people used us was that we were much friendlier than big bookies: you could have a laugh and a joke when you placed your bet, not just be asked for an anonymous account number.

However, the delights of Brighton were becoming a bit boring for me. Every time I went to London I realised how much I really wanted to be back there. I used to go up every Sunday night to play poker at the flat of a friend, Monty Marks. The school used to consist of us two, Monty's flatmate Adrian Jacobs, two Americans – Cy Stewart and Oscar Lerman – and a very young Beatle called Paul McCartney.

I was terribly impressed by Oscar. He was six foot tall with a slow, drawling American accent. He had come to London, he said, to get away from a girl. It proved the right move: later he was to meet Jackie Collins and marry her. But, at the time, he had a swish bachelor pad in Park Lane and was about to open, with Alf Barnett, the Ad Lib, which became one of London's hottest clubs.

The club was just off Leicester Square. You went up to it in a tiny lift and when the doors opened – wow! It was absolutely electric. It seemed that everybody, from the latest pop stars, to the new breed of photographers – Bailey, Duffy and Donovan – to Mary Quant, as well as her top models, would end their evenings there. Her leading model, Jan de Souza, would eventually become my wife.

The galvanising attraction was the manager, Brian Morris, who was also the orchestra leader. He was a real showman and he would stand in the middle of the floor and really get people going, have them feeding out of his hand – bopping around on one leg or down on their knees. Teddy, the black chef with a tall white hat, would come out of the kitchen and dance away with the customers.

Brian was very much in love with Alma Cogan, one of the most popular singers of the time. When she died he left the Ad Lib. The club never recovered, and I don't think Brian did, either.

Oscar Lerman and I became good buddies. I think we both had a similar attitude to the world. My boss had sent me on a course based on Dale Carnegie's book, *How to Win Friends and Influence People* when I was a fashion salesman. I went feeling very cynical but I learnt several things, not least how vital it was to smile and how, more relevantly, the most important thing to someone is the sound of their name. Both seemed to come naturally to Oscar, who cloaked a will of steel in a wonderfully cool, laid-back way.

Over a bottle of Mateus Rosé – one of the fashionable drinks at that time – we would set the world to rights, talk about girlfriends and horses. He thought I was wasting my time in bookmaking and said I should be in the club business. I pointed out that although I could calculate the most advantageous odds to offer on a dog race in a matter of seconds, or assess the amount of material needed to make a hundred coats, I had no knowledge of the nightclub business – not even how to run a bar. But he insisted I could learn quickly and asked if I was interested. Of course I was interested.

It must have been nearly two months after that conversation that I got a call in my Brighton SP office from Oscar. 'Can you come up to London on Thursday? I have a proposition to put to you.'

'Sure,' I said. 'Can you give me some indication what it's about?'

'I'm leaving the Ad Lib,' he said.

'I'm really sorry to hear that,' I told him.

'Well, one door closes and maybe a better one opens.' Oscar was always the optimist.

Two days later I met him at 11 a.m. at 57 Jermyn Street, the very place where I had spent my memorable evening with John Wayne at the Crazy Elephant, which had since closed down.

Although I was early, Oscar was already there with a short man who wore one of those expensive overcoats with a velvet collar. He introduced him to me as his lawyer. We went downstairs into the dark, disused shell that used to be crammed with people and looked around.

'What do you think?' Oscar asked. 'You said you wanted to run a club.'

'You know very well I have no experience,' I protested.

'Yes or no?' he demanded.

There was never any doubt about it. 'Yes.'

Before I knew it his lawyer had opened his smart calf-leather briefcase and I was signing documents.

As we walked back up into the daylight, I asked Oscar, 'Why me?'

He grinned. 'I don't know what it is. You're an ugly-looking git but the girls seem to go for you, the guys like you. You appear to me to get on with everyone – just right for this business.'

'Well, what about the business side?' I asked apprehensively.

He patted me on the shoulder. 'You'll pick it up fast. It's not that hard.'

So that was how Oscar got me into the business. I didn't know, as I stood there with him, that I would remain working in Jermyn Street for the next 38 years.

I trusted Oscar almost blindly and I wasn't wrong. The club was called Dollys. From the word go it was a huge success, taking over the clientele of the Ad Lib, which, unfortunately, had burnt down.

I was able to move my SP office up to London. My old boss, Harold Lee, back in business, asked me if I knew anyone who needed an office. I did. He owned a building in Great Portland Street and offered me one at a ridiculously low rent – something I will always be thankful for.

The opening night of Dollys was a nightmare for me, a real baptism of fire. I stood behind the desk at reception to welcome the members, not knowing who most of them were. With each smile and 'how are you?' I thought to myself: What the hell have I got myself into here?

Among the co-owners of Dollys were a lawyer called Malcolm Fraser and the boxing brothers George and Billy Walker. George also owned a drinking club in the East End which was frequented by – how shall I put it? – not the most savoury of characters. And they wanted to be members of Dollys. That, coupled with the fact that the Crazy Elephant had not been a membership club and ended up being a hang-out for some pretty tough guys, meant that we got more than our fair share of villains turning up at Dollys.

They tended to see it as their divine right that they should come in and would stride past the reception desk and down the stairs. I would be at the bottom and it was my less than enjoyable duty to try to explain to them that they were not welcome.

I reckon I had more fights than when I boxed in the army. Fifteen rounds every other night was not the reason I became manager of a nightclub. So they gave me a minder. He was a black ex-light-heavyweight boxer called Freddie Mac. Freddie cut a very imposing figure with his shaved head (some 35 years before that became fashionable) and a selection of great sixties shirts with high Indian collars and big billowing sleeves.

The girls at reception would buzz down if some of the wrong sorts were giving them any hassle. I would go up, followed by Freddie, and point out that they couldn't come in because they weren't members.

These were not characters who were used to being told what they could do. 'Who's going to stop us, then?' they would inevitably demand. I wouldn't say a word and Freddie would just stand there.

'Well, fuck you,' was the usual response as they turned and left. I rarely had any problems once Freddie was there – although I got my car kicked in a few times.

That's not to say that no villains became members. Successful villains keep themselves out of the Old Bailey and their names out of the newspapers. But they are known to a small coterie of people. We had many rich members – I think it was Dostoevsky who wrote, 'Behind every large fortune lies a crime.'

Curiously I never had a problem with the major villains: they were usually very generous – big spenders and big tippers. It was the small-time guys who caused problems because they always wanted to show their bravado, so they were soon turfed out.

Of course members could bring in whoever they wanted as guests. One night Monty Marks came and told me Reggie Kray was in. He had overheard him say to his host, Danny, that he had been over visiting his brother, Ronnie, who was currently in Wandsworth Prison and had become great friends with Frank Mitchell, the 'Mad Axeman'.

My heart sank as I thought of the prospect of having the Kray twins and their friends as regulars. They had brought their East End business west and deposed Jack Spot, who had thought of himself as lord of the manor in London's West End.

'You've got to get rid of him,' I told Monty.

He looked nervously back at me. 'Are you crazy? You go.'

Neither of us felt overeager to perform that particular task: the Krays had a reputation for torture and murder that was second to none. In the event I just managed to get Danny's attention after Reggie Kray had gone upstairs. 'If you want to retain your membership here', I warned him, 'I would prefer you didn't bring in people like that.'

Danny looked very uncomfortable. 'He forced me,' he said. Nevertheless, he never brought him again.

There was one member, Simon, who was thought by some to be a hit man. It was only a rumour. He was always very well dressed and it seemed to me that he wouldn't say boo to a goose. In fact he took a shine to Oscar and me and made a point of seeking us out and talking to us when he came to the club.

But I think I owe my continued existence to Simon. It was a Thursday night in November. The club was fairly quiet and he came charging down the stairs, quite out of character.

I could see he was sweating as he grabbed hold of me and moved me into a quiet corner. 'I'm putting my life on the line,' he whispered breathlessly. 'I was at a meeting this morning and the message was to get Johnny Gold from Dollys. Have you ever been in the motor business?'

'No,' I said. 'Why?'

He didn't answer but hurriedly picked up the phone at reception and dialled a number. 'I told you. It's not the Johnny Gold from Dollys. Definitely not.'

I heard later that they were looking for a Johnny Gould but that was the last I ever saw of him. He never came back to the club. But if you're still out there, Simon, thanks.

I don't know why I'm dwelling on the crooks; my wife says I have a morbid fascination with them. But Dollys was full to bursting with gorgeous girls, film stars (American, British, French), rock stars (mainly the Beatles and the Rolling Stones, but all the other groups such as the Who), and people from hairdressing, photography, fashion – all the 'in' industries. Plus, of course, young people in more orthodox jobs who just clamoured to become members.

The musical *Hello Dolly!* was an enormous hit at the time and Oscar, with his usual theatrical panache, had decided that a tape of the title song, rendered in 22 different languages, should always be playing at reception. It drove the girls on the desk mad! Louis Armstrong, yes, what a romantic interpretation. But have you ever heard it in Indian? Or Japanese? Once, I assure you, is enough.

Thanks to his initiative we were pioneers when it came to marketing – this was the mid-sixties – and we sold people little rag dolls at a pound a time. They became a cult among our members and their guests; nobody went home without one – except, possibly, Reggie Kray.

An American telephoned me one day in March to say he was from *Time* magazine and they were doing a piece on London nightlife. Could they come and interview me?

I agreed: we had enough competition out there and I wanted to remain ahead of the field. I suggested they arrive at about eleven on Friday night.

When the two *Time* correspondents, a man and a woman, walked down the stairs, the place – as I had anticipated – was alive and jumping with enough famous faces to star in a movie or stage a rock concert.

There was no such thing as a quiet corner that night, but I shouted answers to their questions with the odd interruption from a pretty girl or a pop singer, which did my cause no harm.

They seemed satisfied with what they'd got and, as they were about to leave, one of them said, 'We'll send our photographer down tomorrow night, if that's all right.'

'I'm afraid it isn't,' I replied. 'I don't allow photographers in the club.'

'But I saw David Bailey a moment ago,' the woman protested.

'Not with his camera,' I answered.

Her colleague became a mite aggressive. 'We've got to have photographs of something we're writing about. It's a *Time* magazine rule.'

'Well it's my rule that we never have photographs taken in Dollys,' I replied. 'This is a place that people come to be private. Whether they're well known or not, they don't necessarily wish that people see who they're with. It's just possible that a gentleman might be with someone other than his wife.'

My irony was lost on the American. 'Listen, John,' he said, 'if we don't take photographs here, we don't mention Dollys in the article. Period.'

'Fine,' I said.

He left with the immortal words, 'We could make or break you.'

It would be an understatement to say they were very pissed off. On 15 April 1966 *Time* published its famous cover story: LONDON: THE SWINGING CITY. Inside, it went on:

In this century, every decade has its city and for the sixties, that city is London. There can never have been a better place to be in your teens and twenties. Ever since the Beatles had made it clear that youth culture was here to stay, and the Labour government opted to promote the mood, London has been taken over by successful young people. Artists, models, photographers, rock stars, fashion designers – all are dedicated to serving and dictating the hip young style. Social revolution with its miniskirt and the contraceptive pill isn't for everyone. What America calls the 'baby boom' generation has come out to play, but its mystified elders are clinging desperately to fast-eroding traditions. For the young those 'standards' are merely 'uncool'; morality, totem of the old, is the dirty word now.

Needless to say, they wrote a very glowing tribute about Dollys in the article with the words 'as pictured below'. But the picture of people dancing was, in fact, taken in the club called the Scotch of St James.

Far from 'breaking us', the piece had a galvanising effect on visiting Americans. One night the upstairs girl buzzed down to say that there were a couple of American hardmen on their way down.

By this time we thought we had dealt with most troublemakers and had moved our reception desk downstairs. But these guys, even in the dark of the stairs, looked really rough – broken noses, cauliflower ears, the lot. I was standing by the desk and I remember thinking: Oh, my God.

The shorter of them said to the girl there: 'We've read about this place, we're visiting London and we'd like to come in.'

In her most English way she said, 'I'm terribly sorry but you have to be a guest of a member and also you have to be accompanied by girls.'

The guy who was further from me, obscured by his companion, seemed to accept this. He just turned round and said, 'I'm going back up.'

But the other guy called to him, 'Hey, Rocky, wait a minute.'

A bell went off in my brain. I was ten feet away from one of my heroes. Forty-nine professional fights and never beaten – a record that stands to this day. In 1951 my father and I had listened on the radio as he beat the legendary Joe Louis. When I was in the army in Germany I stayed up all night to listen to him get knocked down in the first round by Jersey Joe Walcott, lose the next seven rounds and then, amazingly, knock him out to become heavyweight champion of the world. It was maybe because I had only heard him on the radio – TV was in its infancy in Britain – that I had failed to recognise him.

I stepped across to him. 'Mr Marciano,' I said hesitantly, 'the young lady is correct in everything she has told you, but if you and your friend would like to join me at my table, we can bend the rules a little.'

He and his friend came in, ordered Cokes and seemed genuinely thrilled to be in the middle of this social London scene. I, on the other hand, was like a schoolboy in making conversation with my idol. He told me how he had first come to England at the very end of the war and had learnt to box as a conscript for Uncle Sam. I was beginning to tell him how I had boxed in the British army but I hadn't progressed quite as far as he had, when, suddenly, Rocky Marciano grabbed my arm.

'Holy shit,' he said. 'I can't believe I am in the same goddam room as Ringo Starr. I've got to get his autograph for my kid.'

'OK,' I said and got up and walked over to Ritchie. He was with his then wife, Maureen.

'Hi, Johnny,' he said. 'Want to join us?'

'I can't,' I replied. 'Ritchie, you know I never bother you but I wonder if you could do an autograph for a guest.'

Automatically, he pulled his pen out of his pocket. 'Sure. Who's it to?'

'The surname's Marciano,' I said, 'but I'm not sure of the boy's first name.'

Ritchie immediately looked across at my table and saw who it was. He leapt to his feet, took Maureen by the hand and told her, 'We're joining Johnny'.

I don't know who was more in awe of whom, Ringo Starr or Rocky Marciano. They had both fought to the top of their respective fields. I think it was a draw – but it was certainly a night to remember.

Chapter Eight

The old-style nightclubs still thrived in London in the mid-sixties – places like the Society, which was also in Jermyn Street, or the 400 Club in Leicester Square, which was really a forerunner of Annabels. There men had to wear a black tie and women wore their pearls and people behaved accordingly.

We were different, reflecting the changes that were taking place in that decade when you didn't have to have a BBC accent to appear on television: anybody from any background with any education could appear, such as Cathy McGowan on the Friday-evening pop programme *Ready Steady Go!* Its war cry was, 'The weekend starts here' and many of those on the programme would end up in Dollys mixing with people ranging from stockbrokers to girls about town.

Of course, the reason a lot of people gravitate to bars, restaurants and clubs, then as now, is because they hope to rub shoulders with the rich and famous. And they seem willing to tolerate their excesses. I remember an incident in Dollys that showed me how celebrities can really get away with all sorts of things. One night Jean-Paul Belmondo was in with Ursula Andress and they were dancing together. I don't know if he thought he was an ice skater or what, but he started to spin her round and round so that she was literally horizontal to the floor.

I rose to my feet in horror praying: 'Please God, don't let him drop her or I'm going to get sued something awful.' At that moment there was an almighty sound of crashing and I couldn't bear to look. When I did, I saw that two very irate guys and two girls – one with a piece of lemon in her hair – had leapt up from their table, where there was the squashed-up body of a woman.

Belmondo looked aghast. The two guys wanting to kill him gazed down at the table and one of them said, 'My God, it's Ursula Andress.'

The girl with lemon in her hair and a very posh accent asked, 'Miss Andress, are you all right?'

If it had been John and Mary Smith, it would have been World War Three!

I make no secret of the fact that I enjoy meeting famous people – I enjoy meeting nonfamous ones, too, but the former are better for attracting customers. At the same time, I always put business first and no name has ever been too big to break the rules and get away with it – as I shall reveal later with regard to George Best, Keith Moon and other problem members.

My first confrontation with a star involved Lawrence Harvey. He was having a drink in Dollys one night with James Hanson and the late Gordon White (rich business partners but not yet lords) and another actor, his great mate John Ireland. Ireland, a Canadian, used to be a swimmer in a water carnival but went on to be nominated for an Oscar for *All the King's Men*. He was known, however, as Mr Chopper and claimed that Dougie Hayward, the esteemed London tailor, had to put an extra gusset in his trousers because he was so well hung. Dougie is one of my oldest friends but such is his professional discretion that he has never passed comment on the matter.

James and Gordon were both members of Dollys and, on this occasion, Hanson settled the bill. A couple of nights later the same four men returned for a drink. This time Hanson and

White had to leave early and Lawrence Harvey and John Ireland stayed on, with Harvey insisting that it was his turn to pay the bill.

The manager of the club then was a Dane called Oscar, a short, nervy man. He came up to me and I could see that his round face was reddened and sweating.

'Mr Gold, I'm really sorry to bother you,' he said, 'but Lawrence Harvey wants to sign the bill.'

'He can't sign the bill,' I told him. 'He's not a member. What are you asking me for?'

'He told me to ask you.'

'Well, go back and tell him the answer's no.'

Reluctantly, Oscar made his way back to the star, only to return in less than two minutes, white as a ghost. 'Mr Gold, I'm really sorry but he's going mad. He's screaming and yelling.'

I was angry. Harvey might be a big movie star – I had adored him in *Room at the Top* and with Elizabeth Taylor in *Butterfield 8* – but he was abusing his status. He was, after all, only Lauruska Mischa Skikne from Lithuania, a good Jewish boy like myself. Or not so good that night.

I strode over to him and asked politely, 'Lawrence Harvey?'

'Yes,' he exploded, somewhat the worse for drink. 'What do you mean I can't sign the bill?'

'You're not a member. If you sign the bill what am I meant to do – send my secretaries out to find where Lawrence Harvey is living or staying so that we can get it paid?'

'You send it to Lawrence Harvey, care of the world,' he snapped back. 'And, at the same time, why don't you just go and fuck yourself?'

'Before I have that pleasure,' I replied, 'perhaps you might like to tell me where you're staying.'

'The Grosvenor House Hotel.'

I took his bill, called over a waiter and handed it to him. 'You will take Mr Harvey's bill to the Grosvenor House Hotel, you will present it to the cashier and you will come back with the cash. Do you understand?'

Harvey was outraged. 'Fuck you,' he yelled as he motioned to John Ireland to get up and go. 'I'm never setting foot in this place again.'

'That is your prerogative,' I told him as he went off, still screaming.

Three days later I walked into Dollys and Harvey was sitting there. He caught my eye and I looked back at him and went over to his table.

'Good evening,' I said.

'I'm sorry about the little upset the other night,' he said. 'I was in the wrong. But I enjoy coming here and I'd like to become a member.'

'It will be my utmost pleasure,' I replied. 'I will arrange the forms. And, by the way, you can sign the bill whenever you like.'

'Thanks,' he grinned.

From then on, the first cheque I used to receive every month from accounts was from Larry Harvey. On the button. We became great friends. When we talked, he would very often reminisce about his days on the stage. He had been in rep in South Africa, where he grew up, and had then come to RADA. His favourite role was Henry V, with which he made an enormous impact at the Old Vic and, later, on Broadway.

But the financial seduction of the movies was too tempting, although he went on to make great films such as *A Dandy in Aspic*. He was one of the founder members of Tramp but he didn't live too long to enjoy it. He died of cancer when he was only 45 – what a waste.

I found myself always naturally relaxed and at ease with people in sport and show business, maybe because they were on my patch. And that in itself probably made them more relaxed – no photographers or reporters. In my experience even the biggest stars in the world can be terribly insecure; if they have a movie that doesn't make it or a record that doesn't sell, they fear they are never going to get another job. I felt I understood most of them and certainly spoke their language.

Less so in the case of Lee Marvin. A member of Dollys, Kenny Hyman, was shooting interiors for his film *The Dirty Dozen* in London in 1966. It was the fictional story of twelve American soldiers, all in prison for rape or murder, who were offered a reprieve if they undertook a suicidal mission into the heart of Germany. Before they set off, it was Lee Marvin's character's task to make them as mean, vicious and ruthless as men can be.

There were rumours in the London gossip columns that some of the actors had found it difficult throwing off their characters after shooting and enjoyed hard drinking and riotous behaviour. So, when Kenny asked me if he could bring his cast down to meet me and see if there was some way they could have a temporary membership of Dollys, I responded with a hardly over-enthusiastic 'fine'.

But they *were* fine – on the first evening, at least. Charles Bronson, Lee Marvin, Ernest Borgnine and Telly Savalas sat at the table mild as pussycats. Robert Webber talked the whole time; James Brown – the legendary Cleveland running back who was making his first movie – kept them amused with locker-room tales; and Trini Lopez – best known for 'If I had a Hammer' – tried out his new song for the film which included the line, 'Such a pretty girl is like a bramble bush'. It didn't go on to be one of his greatest hits.

Not for the first time, the stories in the tabloids had been exaggerations. I told them they were all welcome to use the club while they were in London.

In order to enter the main discotheque in Dollys you had to go through some swing doors. Two nights later they were thrown open and in stumbled Lee Marvin as in *Cat Ballou*, more drunk than any man has a right to be and stay alive. He staggered across the dance floor, tripped over himself, somehow managed to rectify his fall with a somersault and ended up in the lap of David Bailey, who was sitting with his then wife, Catherine Deneuve.

He grabbed Bailey's glass, swallowed the content and mumbled to Catherine, 'Do you know how I like my whisky?'

'No,' she replied, stiffly.

'With the cork out,' Marvin mumbled, before putting his head on their table.

Fortunately, James Brown and Charles Bronson were also in Dollys that night. I said to them, 'Listen, someone's going to give him a right-hander or worse, something dreadful could happen. I suggest you take him out of here.'

I had a feeling they had done it before. They grabbed Lee, half carried, half dragged him upstairs and threw him in a taxi.

Oscar used to be largely unimpressed by the stars at Dollys but Jimmy Brown was something different. I knew of his reputation as America's greatest ever running back, but what I didn't know – until the three of us talked – was quite what an all-rounder he had been. At Syracuse University he was all-American in both football and lacrosse, played for the basketball squad and, as a member of the track team in his second year, finished fifth in the National Decathlon championships.

I found him a very sensitive man. He used to keep a record of all the main moves and how they might have been improved after each game. He was drafted into the Cleveland Browns, but never really got on with the coach, Paul Brown. 'Everyone in this story is a Brown,' Jim remarked ruefully. It came to a head in 1962, when either he or Paul had to go and, unusually, it was the coach. In 1963 Jim had his best season.

He was still regarded in a class of his own when he came to London in the off-season to make *The Dirty Dozen* in 1966. He would talk to me occasionally about how much longer he could stay at the top. As an Englishman, I wasn't best qualified to pass opinions and I think he rather liked that.

But that summer he shocked sporting America by announcing,

from London, that he was quitting the game. He was only thirty but he went on to have a busy career in movies, probably, after Sidney Poitier, the most popular black actor. We kept in touch and I would see him whenever I went to LA. Having grown up in a Long Island ghetto, he became very involved in starting programmes for deprived inner-city children.

The stars didn't come to Dollys for the cuisine – chicken in a basket was our Epicurean delight – and presumably they could get champagne and drinks of equal quality at their hotels. They came for the scene and they came for the girls. Some were content to dance the night away; most were hopeful that they might enjoy even more.

Roman Polanski put it to me more bluntly. 'English girls are the most straightforward in the world. Somehow they let you know immediately whether they are going to sleep with you or not.'

In Roman's case, judging by the fact that he rarely left the club unaccompanied, there can have been very few 'nots'. He was a regular, being resident in London, and making three pictures in succession here: *Repulsion*, *Cul-de-Sac* and the studio sequences of *Dance of the Vampires*.

He was always on his best behaviour when Jill St John came to town. I think they had a genuine affection for each other. This was before she married Jack Jones, dated Henry Kissinger and then remarried Robert Wagner.

Things might have been different if he had been allowed to have Jill as his co-star in *Dance of the Vampires*. He had written it with her in mind as Sarah, the innkeeper's daughter. Jack MacGowran would be the mad professor with Roman himself as his assistant. He had always wanted to do a spoof vampire film and told me, on more than one occasion, that since he came from Poland he had a much better idea of what Transylvania was like than British or American directors.

He complained to me that his producer, Marty Ransohoff, not only didn't want him to act in the movie but kept pushing an

American actress, Sharon Tate, as the Jewish innkeeper's daughter since she was already contracted to the backers, MGM. Roman said, in her hearing, that she looked too wholesomely all-American and not Jewish enough. (Jill St John had been born Jill Oppenheim.)

Sharon, he said, was very upset by this but all the more determined to get the part. She turned up for her screen test in a red wig and clinched the role. MGM also approved of Roman acting in the film.

Sharon was different from most of the girls whom Roman brought in. For a start she addressed the Italian staff fluently in their own language – she had spent part of her childhood there when her father had been some bigwig in the army. And Roman listened to her. Usually he was expounding on his own remarkable past to some wide-eyed girl, but in this instance there seemed to me – from afar – that there was a conversation between equals.

There was one other thing about Sharon: she was breath-takingly beautiful. They were a good couple, constantly together until her career took her back to America to appear in *Valley of the Dolls*.

Dance of the Vampires didn't do much for Roman or Sharon – or for me. He felt there wasn't much of a future for him making films in England and followed her to America. There he had his biggest success, *Rosemary's Baby*.

They returned to England to marry at Chelsea Register Office in January 1968. They celebrated all over London including, of course, at Dollys.

The club certainly fulfilled all the criteria of swinging London but, after a period of deteriorating relations, Oscar Lerman had a series of blazing rows with his main partner, Malcolm Fraser. The two men decided to toss a coin for Dollys. Oscar lost – although, in the long run, he won.

I had a very small stake in the place so it barely affected me, but I owed my job to Oscar and, when he decided to get out, I followed. It was a painful decision. I loved the place and I was aware that I had played a significant part in building it up.

I thanked all the staff who had worked for me and departed, without ceremony, on a Saturday night. I was confident I had left Dollys in good shape: we used to do at least 300 table settings on a Friday night and more than 350 on a Saturday. Once again I was unemployed, but Oscar promised me we would look for premises to buy a club in which I could be his partner.

One Tuesday I was seeing a friend in the City for lunch when Hilary Gerard, a stockbroker who was a regular at Dollys, came over to our table. He had met Ringo Starr at the club and later went to work as his financial adviser, which he still is.

'I haven't seen you at the club for a bit,' he said.

'No, I'm not there any more,' I replied. 'Oscar and I have left.'

'Really? Why?' he enquired.

I shrugged and smiled. 'Just one of those things.'

'Shame,' he said. 'I went in on Friday and there were only about seventy people there, so I went home and came back on Saturday and there can't have been much more than a couple of dozen of us.'

A few days later my telephone rang at home. It was Malcolm Fraser. 'I'm going to sue you for every penny you've got,' he yelled. 'You're stopping people coming to the club.'

'What are you talking about?' I said. 'How can I stop people going to the club? It's not as if I've set up my own place and I'm telling people to come to it. If people ask me why they haven't seen me at Dollys I merely say I've left. No reasons.'

'I know you're up to something,' he screamed. 'And, when I find out, you're going to regret it.'

I didn't say anything. I learnt that he hung on for a bit as attendance continued to decline. It was obviously horrible for him. I felt sad but flattered. The members had not been interested in who owned the place: in their eyes it had always been my club.

Six weeks later Dollys, the darling of the Swinging Sixties, closed down. Some years later Malcolm committed suicide.

Chapter Nine

Oscar and I started to look for other club premises all over London. The best we came across was the old River Club on the Thames Embankment, just across from Dolphin Square. We got financial backing from Richard Burton and Elizabeth Taylor, along with the film producer Elliott Kastner. I did a deal with a friend of mine who owned a company called Bertram Boats and suggested he might like to use the River Club during the day as a showroom in exchange for allowing us to have four speedboats that would be used by club members to go up and down the Thames at night.

It was very exciting. I said to the Burtons, 'Please – when you go back to America – the one thing we don't want is any publicity.' Two minutes after they landed everyone knew we were opening this club. I came back from holiday a week later to discover that Harry Saltzman – the Bond producer – had gazumped us. I was in tears. We'd been working on this for over a year and I was gutted.

We searched everywhere – basements, shells, former churches – for another two years. I was getting really cheesed off; people, especially those who knew me from Dollys, kept asking, 'When are you going to open again?'

I kept saying, 'Don't worry, we'll open.'

Then, out of the blue, I got a call from Al Burnett, the comedian who owned the Stork Club. He used to tell the same jokes every night, which his members seemed to relish. Sunday night at the Stork Club was like a religion – Princess Margaret was always there.

Al said he'd heard I was looking for premises and suggested we take a look at the Society in Jermyn Street, which he co-owned. I'd never been but I knew it was a formal sort of dinner-dance place with a string orchestra and a declining clientele. The Queen Mother was known to go there when she wanted to celebrate one of her horses winning at the races. But those days had passed and the Society was no longer fashionable.

Oscar and I took a look at it the next day. When I got to the bottom of the stairs and stood in the foyer, I punched the air and said, 'Oscar, this is it!'

He looked at me: 'What the hell are you talking about?'

I insisted: 'I'm telling you, this is it.'

We opened the door to where the discotheque is today and there was the beautifully carved seventeenth-century wood panelling and the chandeliers. After we inspected the next room with its incredible zodiac ceiling, Oscar conceded: 'I don't know how you knew without seeing it, but you're right.'

He wanted to call the club 'La Club' so that we could build on the reputation of 'Le Club' in New York and get publicity on that. I didn't agree. We needed a name that was original and snappy and fun – something that might reflect the sort of club we wanted.

I went home and that night on television there was a documentary about Charlie Chaplin. The narrator said 'this was the greatest tramp of all' and, as he said it, it was like an electric shock. Tramp – could be a down-and-out or a hooker or the sound of marching. I loved the idea of the rich panelling and chandeliers and a name that conjured up an image of sawdust on the floor.

I called Oscar immediately and he repeated the word 'Tramp' several times in his broad American accent.

'Yes,' he said eventually, 'that's it.'

We worked for most of 1969 to get the place ready for business. The Society had stately oak walls, which went with its image. I was anxious to preserve them – they remain to this day – but, at the same time, give the place a distinctive style that would encourage members to dance on the tables in the discotheque as opposed to bowing to the Queen Mother when she dropped by.

In August of 1969 I fulfilled a promise I had made to Tony Newley that, if ever he played Las Vegas, I would come and see him. Joan Collins, then his wife, rang and reminded me: 'You're coming to stay with us in Beverly Hills and then we'll go to Vegas.' Which we did, the day I arrived, and by car since Dori Previn (ex-wife of André) was accompanying us and had an extreme aversion to flying.

We all enjoyed the beautiful drive through the dreamscape of the Mojave Desert, ending up in the mock-Roman opulence of Caesar's Palace, where Tony was to play and where I had an endless suite of rooms. I was wide-eyed and thrilled.

Tony went down a treat. He had cleverly studied the Vegas shows and knew just the right combination of strutting his stuff and interconnecting with the audience to offer.

We had a wonderful time. Every night we used to go and see a different show. One particular evening, Joan said, 'Good news, we're going to see Elvis tonight.' I was not a great fan – I preferred the Stones and the Beatles – so I gracefully declined. This was not something Joan would accept. 'Oh, come on, we're going, stop being a boring old fart.' So I got dragged to see Elvis.

Never have my preconceptions changed so immediately. He was utterly fantastic. It wasn't just a performance: it was the experience of being in the same room as a consummate performer, who in a subtly astute manner managed to take the mickey out of himself and still be worshipped. I went mad with the rest of the audience, standing on the table and hollering for more.

I was woken the following morning by an early call from an unusually sombre-voiced Tony Newley. 'Can you come over to the suite as soon as you can?'

I scrambled into my clothes and went across. Tony had left the door ajar and Joan was on the phone.

'Have you heard the news?' he asked.

I was mystified: 'No, what?'

'Sharon's been murdered.'

I said, 'You're joking – what are you talking about?'

'They've just announced it on the news. Some other people have been murdered too and they don't know who they are.'

I racked my brains trying to think whether Roman was in the country. I didn't know. What I did know was that his wife was pregnant with their first child. And she could have been with other friends of ours, if not her husband.

Joan, Dori and I packed quickly and set out for LA. Tony would fly in later for the funeral. We drove in silence, our ears attuned only to the 24-hour news station, which slowly unravelled the grim details. There were no official statements to begin with but the station listened to the police short-wave transmissions. The news was eked out bit by bit: there were four other victims: Wotjek Frykowski, his girlfriend Abigail Folger, Jay Sebring (the hairdresser who was Sharon's former lover and now was always with the Polanskis) and Steven Parent had also been murdered.

What was ugly about the reporting of the story was the implication that they had all been at some party, orgy even, high on drugs and – would you believe it? – practising black magic.

The newspapers had a field day, trying to link Roman's dark films with the fact that there was a hood found over Sebring's head and he was tied to Sharon by a rope. (It wasn't true –

although Jay's reputation as a man fond of bondage had some foundation.) *Time* magazine revealed that one of Sharon's breasts had been cut off and an X had been cut on her stomach. They were determined to turn the victims into a cult of sorts. Abigail Folger was described as an aimless heiress; she was indeed rich but she was also a daily social worker.

The night before the funeral there was a wake of sorts with Brian Morris, who at that time was running a club in LA, myself, Peter Lawford, Jack Nicholson and Warren Beatty (who, with Victor Lownes of *Playboy*, had escorted a sedated Roman Polanski back from England). I can't remember where we went. It was a very narrow bar and we all got very, very drunk.

The following day I went to the funeral with my good friends Leslie and Evie Bricusse – Leslie wrote with Tony Newley at the time. The first thing we saw when we got to the outside of the church was Kirk Douglas giving a photographer a right hand. The Hollywood community was up in arms about the rumours that had been spread so unfairly in the press.

It was a very moving ceremony. I adored Sharon; she was the most beautiful girl. Afterwards we all went back to the house of Bob Evans, the producer of *Love Story*, who lost his wife, Ali McGraw, to Steve McQueen. He used his huge pool house for drinks. I was standing there talking to Evie Bricusse. I had seen Roman at the service but he had not seen me. Now suddenly he spotted me across the room. He came across and we put our arms around each other.

'Johnny, Johnny, you were there, you were there,' he wept.

I thought: Blimey, what does he mean I was there? At the murders?

He started sobbing like a baby. 'You were there, Johnny, when I met her in Dollys.'

The whole thing was a fairly unbelievable scene. Suddenly they were saying, 'All those ready for Act Two' – the funerals of the others who were murdered.

The LA police always assumed it was a drug-related murder because they believed that Wotjek Frykowski dabbled in that scene. Roman was intent on finding the killers and, against police advice, put up a $25,000 reward for information leading to their arrest. It was lucky that he did: three months later a woman called Susan Atkins boasted to a fellow prisoner of the Manson family's exploits. The fellow prisoner was in need of money, told the cops and Charles Manson was arrested.

Life returned to a sort of stunned normality. One day I phoned George Hamilton, with whom I had become friendly when he was over in London making a less than wonderful movie. He said, 'Johnny, I can't believe you're here. It's my birthday tomorrow, you've got to come. It's at the Candy Store.'

I told him I was with Joan and Evie and he insisted that I bring them. So we went to the Candy Store. It was packed; you couldn't move. All Hollywood was there. I was sitting on a stool nursing a drink when suddenly I was lifted right up in the air.

The place fell silent – no one was more silent than I was. My attacker announced, 'This man made me feel like a fucking king when he didn't know who I was. He didn't know who I was and he made me feel like a king.' And I was paraded round the place, until he put me down and kissed me.

It was Jimmy Brown and everyone was looking a little apprehensive, not to say terrified. At that particular time he was getting a lot of bad publicity for being antiwhite (beating up white guys in the car park) and so to see Jimmy kissing and cuddling a white guy was completely out of character.

Joan had said when I arrived that she wanted to give a party in my honour at her house and asked for the names of people I'd like to invite. I had put the name of Jimmy down. But she told me we couldn't have Jimmy Brown because she'd read all about his exploits. He later joined us at our table at George's birthday and Joan leant over to me and whispered, 'If you want to invite him to the party, it's all right.'

So Jimmy came to the party with Lola Fallana, the exotic dancer, and I was with a pretty English nanny whose name, for the life of me, I cannot remember. Lots of stars were there. Jimmy suggested, 'Johnny, let's do a swap. I love your nanny.' And I said, 'Well, I love Lola, but I don't think Lola's going to stand for me after you.'

That proved to be the case, which was probably just as well. Follow Jimmy? Wow!

Back in Britain the club was beginning to look promising. Bill and Oscar tried to keep the refurbishment within a reasonable cost and I wrote to all the people whom I wanted to be our founder members – most of them friends or established acquaintances – ranging from Mick Jagger to Princess Margaret and most of the members of Dollys. We opened Tramp with about three hundred members, not a lot. The letter asking people to join just said, 'Tramp will be open for normal business on 18 December.'

So five months after man first set foot on the moon, four months after the Queen's investiture of the Prince of Wales, three months after Biba became a department store, two months after the BBC transmitted the first edition of *Monty Python's Flying Circus*, one month after the Rolling Stones first played Madison Square Garden in New York and thirteen days before the sixties came to an end, Tramp opened in the now refurbished basement of the Society at 40 Jermyn Street, London SW1 – the street that houses a succession of exclusive men's shirt shops and remains a centre of the Masonic movement. In fact the premises once had a secret passage where King Edward VII, a fervent Mason, could be smuggled in and out.

I won't forget that evening in a hurry. At 9 p.m. on Thursday

18 December 1969, my partners, Oscar Lerman and Bill Ofner, and I stood by the bar to drink to our new venture. They seemed calm, although both were smoking furiously. I certainly was as nervous as hell. Suppose nobody showed. There had been no publicity and there was no party on offer, not so much as a free drink.

Opening any new business is always nerve-racking but somehow clubs and restaurants seem more so.

I looked around our staff, all fashionably smart, waiters in white polo-necks and managers in blue blazers. They were headed by Louis and his assistant, a very shy and retiring young man called Guido, who took over managing the club and has remained to this day. Someone once told him he looked like Alain Delon and he hasn't let me forget since.

I was unmarried in those far-off days and quite slim – a shape that has not remained to this day. I had been having a romance with a top Mary Quant model, Jan de Souza, a strikingly beautiful girl, Portuguese-Indian by birth. But we had had a stupid row and she had gone to live in Australia.

So we stood there – waiting. It was 9.15 – nobody! Then it began. As Kevin Costner (a future Tramp habitué) was later to say in *Field of Dreams*: 'If you call them, they will come.'

And they did, including Natalie Wood and Jeremy Lloyd and, of course, Jackie Collins, Oscar's wife. Michael and Shakira Caine turned up. So did Peter Sellers and Leslie Bricusse and Richard Harris.

Although it wasn't overpacked, lots of people were arriving, but I wouldn't let them in because they weren't members. Membership was £10.50. And those people who paid £10.50 more than thirty years ago still pay £10.50 today because we keep them at the same annual fee they originally paid. When I look at the bank statements and I see 'Sultan of Brunei: £10.50', I cry!

Everybody had a great time – we all did. It was an incredible night, like the opening of a show that you knew was going to be a hit.

Jackie Collins once wrote of Bill, Oscar and me: 'From the first day we opened they were triplets in tune, never getting in each other's way, always working to make Tramp the best and most fun club in town.'

I won't contradict that.

Chapter Ten

We were up (late the next day with very sore heads) and running. In that little burst of activity before Christmas word went out that there was a new kid on the block.

On the outside I wanted the club to remain understated to the point of anonymity. Millions of people have walked along Jermyn Street without noticing the low-key bronze plaque with the simple word 'Tramp' on it.

If you are positioned right, refusal to seek publicity can be the most potent attraction – something the Saatchi brothers later practised to perfection.

Demand for membership didn't just soar: it spread like an uncurbed virus. I never realised I had so many friends. There was a downside to this: one or two or more people were a little disaffected not to be invited to join.

I never liked making people members without physically seeing them. Once we were open, then members would come in with guests. Often the guests might ask to become a member. As word started to filter out that Tramp was a kind of a cool place, more and more people began to ask for membership. But I was always mindful of the mix.

At the time Charles Clore was one of the richest men in London, very powerful and influential. One evening he came up to me and said, 'Gold, I want you to make a friend of mine a member.'

I replied, 'Forget about it, Charlie.'

He glared at me: 'What do you mean "forget about it"?'

I said, 'Let me ask you a question – you enjoy coming here with your pretty young girls, right?'

He agreed: 'Yeah.'

'Well, how would you feel if a bunch of old farts like you were sitting along there, all alongside you with young girls?'

Clore grinned: 'I'd hate it.'

'Good. So don't ask me to make any of your friends members.'

That was my philosophy: I wanted to be very exclusive. I suppose really I'm a snob. I just wanted a combination of people and nationalities who were going to mix together. I didn't want to see the room full of ugly people and old millionaires. I wanted it to be a very pretty room with the right people. That was my vision of Tramp.

My staff and even my partners got pissed off with me. But money was never my motivation. I really loved and enjoyed what I did and I really enjoyed my clientele. I got a terrific buzz out of them. I loved meeting these people. I loved seeing them have a great time. I loved the fact that Warren Beatty could walk in and feel totally at ease. I loved the fact that Kirk Douglas and these heroes of mine were in my room. It was something special to me. The staff thought they were working for a lunatic.

But I guess this could be why we went on to last for thirty years. If money had been the motivation, we couldn't have lasted as long as we did because it would have been a different scene. Arab princes offered me £5,000 and more in cash for membership. But I wouldn't take it.

Bill Ofner, to say the least, erred on the side of the economical. He believed in buying only second-hand kitchen equipment. 'It'll save us a fortune,' he insisted. 'Most restaurants buy the stuff brand-new and then they go bankrupt in six months.' He had a point – but we haven't gone bankrupt, at least not at the time of writing, 32 years later.

But we did buy all these second-hand things. People used to laugh at us. Oscar and I insisted, however, that the food be of the top quality. Before the hamburger boom hit London we served the best hamburgers – and the best steaks, grilled sole, asparagus and smoked salmon. It was the sort of food I loved: nothing fancy-schmancy. (Funnily enough, it's coming back into favour in America at the moment after the fad for modern cuisine. The hottest restaurant in New York is the Canteen and it is serving pretty well our original menu.)

Bill's parsimony was such that when we started we used to work on a shoestring. It was a joke. I had one girl working in the office doing the membership and two bookkeepers and that was that. I still had my bookmaking business and we were taking phone bets during the day. So it was a nonstop, 24-hour business. I never stopped, unless I fell asleep at my desk. Then the phone would go: 'We've got a flood'; 'The chef hasn't turned up – he's drunk'; 'There's an inspector coming round'. In the catering business every day brings a fresh disaster.

It really was a false economy. If we had had two girls doing the membership and we had put it on a computer when it should have been on a computer, the membership renewals would have gone out on time and it would have more than paid for itself. But we were very content and carefree and, to be honest, lucky.

I was just happy doing what I was doing and I wanted my customers to be happy doing what they were doing, and the staff to be happy. They were trained, they knew their jobs but they weren't under any strict directions – no 'don't do this or that'.

There was a very pertinent reason for this. When people come to a club, there's nothing worse than if they feel uptight, which they can do if the staff are uptight. It's important to me that the club should have a natural feeling. When you come to choosing the membership, the most important thing is to have a good mix of people. It's not dissimilar to having a party at your house: you don't want people of all the same ilk or backgrounds or doing the same sort of work. That would be a bore. It's the same with a club – you want people who are able to mix, and that's when you get this wonderful party atmosphere. If it's not a party every night, you're in trouble.

There was no doubt about it that one of the greatest attractions was to rub shoulders with the stars or at least say you saw them. And few were bigger than the Beatles or the Rolling Stones, all of whom were loyal to me from my days at Dollys and liked to come to Tramp. I had engineered it that they should sit at either end of the discotheque because I didn't want to mix them all up. There was a healthy rivalry between the two groups – young people's mummies didn't like Stones and they were proud of that – but socially they got on well and John and Paul were guests of honour at Mick's 25th-birthday party.

In those early days, Paul was with Jane Asher – all the Beatles fell for her after she did a TV interview with them. She was so stylish and classy and unobtainable. But, of course, John and Ringo were married. Cynthia Lennon was one of the nicest girls I ever met, down to earth and caring. Ringo was always with his wife, Maureen. He would put two cigarettes in his mouth to light hers for her. And George would sit there holding hands with Pattie Boyd.

Jan and I went on holiday with Ringo and Maureen to the South of France. Neither of them had been there before. When we got to the Hôtel du Cap it was brimming with Hollywood stars. Ringo assumed it was like this all the time but I had forgotten the Cannes Film Festival was on. We had a wonderfully juvenile time.

'So this is how the rich live, Johnny,' Ringo observed.

'Very few of them have as much money as you, Ritchie,' I pointed out.

I once asked John Lennon what it was like watching people

dance to his own music and he drily replied, 'I just try and calculate the royalties you have to pay us, Johnny.'

The Stones, as I mentioned, sat at the other end of the disco. Mick, when he wasn't with Marianne Faithfull, had an eye for a pretty girl and Bill Wyman was fancy-free and fairly predatory. The most introspective and, in a way, the most fascinating was Brian Jones. He was a thinker and a great musician. He was a former choirboy who had been to a public school and romantically had acquired the house where AA Milne wrote *Winnie the Pooh*.

But, by the end of the sixties, the old order had changed. The Beatles had recorded their last album together, *Abbey Road* – which was where Paul and I both lived. The cover, as I'm sure you recall, was of the four of them crossing Abbey Road on a zebra crossing. There was a Volkswagen in the background with the registration '28 IF' – one of the many clues American fans used to convince themselves Paul was dead, despite his appearance on the album cover, since this would have been his age *if* he had lived.

But he wasn't dead: he was in Tramp. Not with Jane Asher any longer but with his new love, Linda Eastman. John had left Cynthia (which made everyone who knew them as a couple really upset) and had moved on to public 'bed-ins' for peace with Yoko Ono, which gave him less time for coming to the club, although he went through periods of turning up. And Ringo was on the verge of breaking up with Maureen.

All of the Beatles were changed somewhat from the nervous boys who had first entered the Ad Lib. Accompanied by Mia Farrow, they had been to India to visit Maharishi Mahesh Yogi and study meditation and spiritual regeneration.

Tragically, Brian Jones, who had founded the Rolling Stones, *was* dead. He had been found lying in his swimming pool that summer, just two weeks after being fired from the band. At an incredible gathering of nearly half a million people in Hyde Park, the Stones had played for free and Mick read a poem to Brian: 'Peace, peace! He is not dead, he doth not sleep. He hath awakened from the dream of life...' Marianne later told me she had found it in Shelley's poem 'Adonais'.

The day after Tramp opened she and Mick were up before Marlborough Street Magistrates, charged with possession of cannabis. For no particular reason Marianne was acquitted but Mick was fined £200.

It wasn't just the Beatles and the Stones: the Who, too, livened the place up – if it needed enlivening. Too much on some occasions: as I will relate in a later chapter I had, unfortunately, to ban their explosive drummer, Keith Moon, from the club.

Rod Stewart became such a good friend that he used to lend me his house for holidays – a most generous man. And visiting American singers, among them Streisand and Sinatra, would come by when they were in town.

I had two tables that were mine: downstairs to the right in the restaurant and to the left in the discotheque, both by the entrance. That way I could greet people and be quickly at the entrance if there was any trouble – which there rarely was.

We made it a rule that all men should be accompanied by a woman so that nobody could regard the club as a 'pick-up' place. However, I was in the fortunate position of being able to invite anybody to join me at my table and in that way I met some fascinating people, usually friends of friends. Even after she joined, Liza Minnelli would always sit with me and insisted I come to her concert at Wembley to give her confidence on the night she knew Barbra Streisand was going.

All rules, however, are made to be bent and not just for famous faces. Dodi Fayed, for instance, had been a friend since I was at Dollys and he was at Sandhurst. He preferred to come unaccompanied – except for a bodyguard, later Trevor Rees-Jones, who survived the Paris tragedy. He would sit at a nearby table.

I was first introduced to Dodi by his father because

Mohammed and his brother, Sala, used to come to Dollys. Dodi was eighteen and an army cadet.

Mohammed asked, 'Can you keep an eye on him for me, Johnny?'

I said, 'Of course, I will.'

Dodi couldn't wait to rush to Dollys every weekend. One particular night he started hitting on this girl and the girl was coming back on him.

He said, 'Oh, Johnny, she's great!'

I replied, 'Dodi, she's not for you. Will you do me a favour? Just stay away from her.'

That puzzled Dodi. 'Johnny, what's the matter with you?'

I told him, 'Well, if you must know, your father's fucking her.'

It was true. Dodi and I became very close friends. I was upset by a lot of the reports about Dodi when he died – things about his being a drug addict and a playboy. It was true that, when he was young, he did get involved in that Hollywood scene – he financed *Chariots of Fire*. I used to go over there because Oscar and Jackie moved there in 1981 and Jan and I used to go and stay with them. We'd get invited to these Hollywood parties (this was before Jackie wrote *Hollywood Wives*) and after dinner there'd be a bowl of coke on the table. That was dessert. If people wanted to, they'd have it and, if they didn't, they didn't. It was part and parcel of the whole scene.

Dodi had his idiosyncrasies at Tramp. If he got up and went to the loo, when he came back to his table he would order a waiter to take away his drink – usually vodka – and replace it with another one. He feared that his drink might be spiked for some reason.

Once, on Jan's birthday, we were having a dinner in Tramp and invited Dodi to join us. I hadn't told him the reason. He said, 'Oh, Jan, I didn't realise it was your birthday.' And he took off this beautiful gold Cartier chain from around his neck and he gave it to her. She wears it virtually all the time – her favourite piece and she loves it. But that was Dodi. Tour guides who stop outside Tramp during the daytime with American tourists tell this story. I never knew how they found out.

Because nothing ever got into the papers about what happened in the club, so not only the stars but also the royals made great use of it. Peter Sellers was a great fan of the club and became a friend, too. He would bring Princess Margaret and Tony Snowdon. Margaret, like Princess Anne, loved to dance. Occasionally, if Tony was working late, Peter and Margaret might come *à deux*. I don't think anything untoward ever went on between the two of them; from my observation they were genuinely just good friends.

Pete was a case. I remember him grabbing Margaret and dancing round the foyer with her in an old-fashioned waltz. She was quite taken aback but she and Tony obviously adored him.

Me, too. Although I think he was just about the most eccentric man I ever met.

Chapter Eleven

Peter Sellers always had a crush on Princess Margaret and, to an extent, it was reciprocated. At one stage he even offered to swop wives with Tony Snowdon but, although the delectable Britt Ekland was on offer, the noble photographer declined.

Despite his overweening talent – Sellers was already a major British star after *The Goon Show* and now an international one after the Pink Panther films – he was in awe of Lord Snowdon professionally. He loved his layouts in the *Sunday Times* and *Paris Match* and they would spend hours discussing photographic equipment and Peter would spend thousands buying the latest lenses.

He was an accomplished photographer himself and got commissioned by *Vogue* to do photoshoots of children of stars such as Michael Caine and Stewart Granger.

He even took pictures of our children, Nicky and Claire. Although they may not have been famous enough for *Vogue*, I keep and treasure them to this day as memories of a remarkable friend.

Like me, he was immensely fond of Ringo and, in the year Tramp opened, cast him in *The Magic Christian*, in which Peter was the richest man in England, Sir Guy Grand, who adopted an impoverished dropout (R Starr). Despite the presence of Raquel Welch, the film did not prove to be a huge international success.

My eyes would light up whenever Peter came into the club: he always had a stream of stories, which he would more re-enact rather than merely tell. He was, of course, very close to Spike Milligan from *Goon Show* days. They were like suicide mates because they both used to suffer from a depression and one would go rushing to the other when he was low. Peter at one time was living in Victoria and he phoned Spike and pleaded with him to come over.

Spike, fearing the worst, pulled his coat over his pyjamas and was at Peter's house in minutes. When he got there, Peter – perfectly OK – said to him, 'I'm pleased you're here. You know, I've bought this new Rolls-Royce and I want you to do me a favour. Come downstairs with me.' They went downstairs and Peter said: 'I've got a squeak somewhere and it's driving me crazy. If you get into the boot, Spike, I'll get the car out and rock it and you'll be able to hear where the squeak is.'

It was two o'clock in the morning but Spike reluctantly agreed and got in the boot. Peter started up the car – 'brrm, brrm, brrm, brrm' – when a copper came by.

He didn't recognise Peter and he enquired: 'Hello, what's going on here?'

Peter started to explain: 'Oh, nothing, officer, I'm just trying to find a little – '

Then the sound of banging came from the boot with a voice shouting: 'Let me out, let me out.'

The copper immediately thought it was a kidnapping. He arrested Peter, summoned reinforcements on his radio and then opened the boot. Out came Spike Milligan, yelling, 'What the fuck's going on, you insane bastard?'

He climbed out and the cop just looked at these two adults who had been playing games with a brand-new Rolls. Fortunately, the two cops in the police car that turned up were Goon fans.

Peter could make me laugh more than anybody I ever met

before or since. We got the giggles in an Indian restaurant one
night and we had to leave – we couldn't eat our food. We had to
ask them to make it a takeaway and went back to Roebuck
House, where he was living then. He had a huge telescope with
which he used to scan the gardens of Buckingham Palace, which
his apartment overlooked. He said it was better than television.
Prince Charles, who was mad about the Goons, would come and
visit him. You could see he was absolutely in awe of Peter.

The late sixties, as you may by now have gathered, was not the
best of time for marriages. Peter and Britt Ekland were no
exception. Fuelled, perhaps, by Peter's experimentation with soft
drugs, they rowed and fought and eventually divorced.

There had been a 23-year-old publicity assistant on *The Magic
Christian* called Miranda Quarry, the stepdaughter of a former
Conservative minister, Lord Mancroft. Peter fell for the upper-
class girl and had an intermittent affair with her. He was actually
in tax exile in Ireland at the time, so it had to be intermittent.

But in August 1970, now divorced from Britt, he married her
in a quiet ceremony in Caxton Hall. The best man was Peter's
odd-job man, Bert Mortimer, and the bridesmaids were Miranda's
Pekingese, Tabitha and Thomasina. It was followed by a less than
quiet celebratory lunch party with (among others) Princess
Margaret and Lord Snowdon, Warren Beatty and his sister,
Shirley MacLaine, Brian Forbes and Nanette Newman, Peter's
daughter, Sarah, me and, bizarrely enough, Peter's ex-wife Britt
Ekland. Peter and Spike Milligan busked on the Knightsbridge
pavement afterwards and actually raised ten shillings.

Peter had poured his heart out to me one night after he had
become engaged to Miranda. He had caught her with somebody
else and he was heartbroken. He came and sat with me and went
through all sorts of traumas. But, once they had got back
together and were married, he insisted: 'Now Johnny, I want you
to come on our honeymoon.'

I said, 'I'm not coming on your honeymoon.'

He was genuinely surprised. 'Why not? I'll have the boat and everything.' I told him I was going on holiday with Leslie Bricusse because he had separated from his wife, Evie, with whom he was having a major row.

So Leslie and I arrived at the Voile d'Or in Cap Ferrat, where Leslie had his boat – a wonderful old Riva speedboat with all the original wood, like a classic Rolls-Royce. On it we found a note from Peter saying, 'Come and join us around the bay at Villefranche.'

Now a man famous for designing ties, but who shall remain nameless, had given me a big white envelope to take to Peter and Miranda as a wedding gift. He had scrawled across it, 'Congratulations, Happy Marriage. Lots of love.'

So we put on our swimming trunks and jumped into Leslie's boat. I grabbed the envelope and put it on the dashboard and we set off from Cap Ferrat to go to Villefranche – only the next bay down. As we zoomed around the headland, going full pelt into the bay, there was a loud 'honk, honk'. It was the customs and police boat. They pulled us over and demanded to see the registration of our boat. Leslie was a bit worried: 'It's in the hotel,' he told them. 'I don't have it here.'

'What documents have you got?' they demanded. They were being very aggressive and really giving us a hard time.

I whispered to Leslie, 'What the fuck's going on? Who do they think we are, smugglers or something?'

An inspector snapped at me, 'What did you say?'

I replied, like a schoolboy, 'Nothing.'

But it looked for a while as if they were going to take us in for questioning and maybe arrest us.

Things had become very uncomfortable when I looked towards the shore and I suddenly saw, standing at the rail of a yacht, Peter and Miranda with Roger and Louisa Moore, all in hysterics, rolling about. I completely broke up, but Leslie didn't immediately see the funny side. I told him, 'Leslie, don't get uptight.' Soon everybody was just creasing themselves, customs and police as well, whom Peter had set up to give us a hard time.

We sped across to Peter's boat, which was called the *Bobo*. We got on board and there was more laughter and kisses and cuddles. I said, 'Oh, by the way, a friend sent you this', and gave them the envelope. We all had lunch – asparagus, lobster, strawberries and a little wine. It was a fabulous day. At the end Peter asked, 'Where are you staying?' I told him the Voile d'Or and he announced that he and Miranda would come and stay as well.

That night Leslie was on the phone, continuing his argument with Evie in California, and I was just relaxing with a book (we had adjoining rooms). Suddenly my phone rang. 'Johnny, come up at once, come up to the penthouse at once.'

It was Peter with a strangulated voice. I shouted out to Les, 'I've got to go to Peter, something's wrong.' I charged up to their room, burst in and there was Peter, with his eyeballs out on stilts.

Peter croaked, 'What the fuck was in the envelope?'

I said, 'I have no idea. I was just the messenger.'

But it was obviously some acid or designer drug. He had taken it and was in the most terrible state.

There was also this strange American in their room (I had no idea where he came from) and he said, 'Quick, we've got to play them some slow music.'

I knew Leslie had a sound system. So we went down to his room where Leslie was now screaming on the phone to Evie, the row to end all rows, and the composer watched helplessly as this American started to remove his precious sound system. It was like a French farce gone mad. But, thankfully, after about 24 hours, Peter was fine. I still have no idea whether the music brought him down.

Peter liked the South of France so much he bought a house there in Port Grimaud, not far from St Tropez. The port was like Venice and you literally had your boat outside your house.

Peter, of course, was captain of some enormous craft, which he was almost wholly incapable of controlling. I was on board once when he banged into a Frenchman as he tried to get it off a mooring. There they were, yelling and screaming, swearing at each other, just like a scene from a Pink Panther movie.

Peter would phone me from his dressing room when they were making those Panther movies. He was a real giggler and loved to try out the lines:

'Your dog is beautiful, does he bite?'

'No, my dog does not bite.'

So he goes to stroke it and the dog bites him.

'You told me your dog didn't bite.'

'That is not my dog.'

He'd be killing himself laughing about these lines in the movie.

The marriage to Miranda did not weather the test of time. By 1973 the first item on the BBC television news was Peter announcing that he was going to marry Liza Minnelli. He was 47, twenty years older than she was, and, unfortunately, still married to Miranda. Actually I thought they made a brilliant couple – both of them so electric with vitality. But it was a short-lived affair and the actress, Lynne Frederick, became his fourth wife and nursed him in his final years as his heart gave up on him. He died aged 54 – far too young. A light went out in the lives of all who knew him.

American stars I had known at Dollys almost automatically transferred their allegiance to Tramp. I have never become blasé about meeting or breaking bread with the major names in Hollywood. None of them got there by accident. They are in some indefinable way different from the rest of us. Whether it is their acting talent or their personality, nobody becomes a star by accident.

There were basic rules I strictly enforced at Tramp to make sure well-known names could enjoy the club in a relaxed way: no autographs, no cameras and no press. It has now worked well for more than thirty years.

By and large our membership is not composed of stargazers: they are getting on with their own nights out. Of course people tend to glance, perhaps more than once, at a famous face but that's sufficient for them to be able to mention at work the next day that they were sitting at the next table to Burt Lancaster the night before.

The only time when there was a tangible reaction to a star was very early on. Steve McQueen walked the length of the dining room. Every head turned and, I promise you, one woman dropped a knife and another a spoon. That guy was the epitome of cool – a short, beautiful man with an almost visible charisma.

As you walk down the stairs of the club you come down to the foyer, to the left of which there's a little couch, which is by the ladies' toilet. The first time Sinatra came into Tramp was with Jill St John (and his faithful minder, Gilly Rizzo, who became a pal). For some reason Sinatra insisted he wanted to sit on that couch and have his drink.

I thought: Holy shit, everyone's going to come down those stairs, see him sitting there, and there's going to be a problem.

I had a chat with him but he seemed quite happy with where he was and, of course, people coming down the stairs that night nearly tripped over themselves.

But there was no incident – save one. Later in the evening he asked me to join them for a drink. We were chatting away and Sinatra observed, 'You know, kid, I really like this club, it's got a great feel. But that light is a bastard.' And he pointed to the chandelier above his head.

I, quick as a flash, replied, 'Yes, I know. I'm sorry, but the dimmer burnt out tonight and we haven't had a chance to replace it.'

This, of course, was total bullshit: we didn't have a dimmer.

He nodded. 'Oh, I see.'

I assured him it would be fixed the next day. The following

morning I phoned up Oscar and told him Sinatra had been in the night before.

'Great, what did he think?'

I told him he loved it apart from the light and that I was going to put in a dimmer.

My partners, as I have said, did not like spending unnecessary money on the club. Oscar said, 'Dimmer? Are you kidding? We'll spray the bulbs pink.'

And for the next 28 years, until we refurbished Tramp, that light remained sprayed pink.

Frank used to come to the club quite frequently when he was in London – very often with my old girlfriend Marion Ryan and her husband, Harold Davidson.

Every year on 4 July Michael Caine gave an American Independence Day party and one year Frank went along. I remember that one especially because my dear friend Terry O'Neill, the photographer, launched into a public, loud and wholly unmelodic rendering of 'My Way' in front of the legendary crooner. Unlike Queen Victoria, Frank was amused.

Sinatra was to become a great friend of Roger Moore, who would often stay with him at his house in Palm Springs.

I had met Roger in the early sixties at a party given by Alfie Marron, a small gay Jewish tailor who was very fashionable in show business circles. We formed a sound friendship. Roger already had made his mark in TV series such as *Ivanhoe*, and I watched his career flourish when he became the Saint.

As I have mentioned, 1969 was a year of marital change. Roger was no exception. His divorce from Dorothy Squires finally came through and he married Louisa Mattiloli, an Italian film star. And Jan, who caught the bouquet at the wedding, as is the tradition, went on to become my wife. Thank God.

Harry Saltzman, who managed to buy the River Club ahead of Oscar and me (it never really thrived as a club), made the wiser decision to cast Roger as James Bond in *Live and Let Die*. The film was a hit and an international star was born. What distinguished Roger's Bond from those of the others who played the part is a sense of humour as dry as his martini and an inimitable twinkle in his eyes.

And that's very much him in real life. He once told me how he observed that the durable Hollywood leading men, such as John Wayne, Gary Cooper and Cary Grant, kept very much the same character throughout their careers. Although he didn't take acting seriously enough to put himself in a category such as theirs.

He was a great friend of Michael Caine – Roger's father was a London policeman and Michael came from the Old Kent Road. Both of them beat the system. I was fortunate enough to spend several holidays with them both, which were inevitably hilarious. Roger acquired a house near the picture-book St Paul de Vence, where hotly disputed games of boules took place in the village square.

I always remember walking down Bond Street with Roger and Michael on a summer day after lunch. A young couple were walking towards us. But between us and them was some scaffolding, so Roger and Michael separated and I fell behind. When the couple passed me one said to the other, 'Did you see? That was Roger Moore.' And the other one said, 'No it wasn't, it was Michael Caine.' And they continued arguing the point as they walked on, much to the amusement of the three of us.

Some stars integrated on the disco floor. One such was the Lebanese-Egyptian, Michael Shalhouz, later better known as Omar Sharif and famous for his roles in David Lean's *Lawrence of Arabia* and *Dr Zhivago*.

He had a very close French friend called Bernard. Omar was in the club one night, and I asked him, 'How come you're by yourself?'

He replied with that devastating smile, 'I'm waiting for Bernard. He's coming with two beautiful girls.'

I said, 'Well, good luck.'

So we had a drink together and eventually Bernard arrived

with these two pretty girls. Omar drained his drink, said he'd see me later and went off into the discotheque with them. I walked in about half an hour later and Omar was dancing away with this bird, cheek to cheek, stroking her hair, the whole scene. He looked at me and winked. Inevitably, later on, he left the club with the girl.

The following night Omar came running down the stairs and said, 'Have you seen Bernard?'

I told him I hadn't.

But he was white with rage: 'I'm going to kill that bastard.'

I asked, 'What's the matter?'

He said, 'You know I left with that girl last night. I took her back to my suite at the Dorchester. As soon as we got in she couldn't get her clothes off quick enough. Into bed. Wonderful. But I couldn't make her come. When a woman goes to bed with me, she's got to have an orgasm. It's a matter of pride. We go on for hours, my body is aching, my tongue is going to fall off, my face is grey, I'm exhausted. I'm doing everything I've ever done to a woman and nothing, nothing. By seven in the morning, I've got to give up. I'm dead. I say, "I'm sorry my dear, I'm exhausted." And she says in her slightly Cockney accent, "Don't worry. I've got to go anyway. Just give me the hundred and fifty pounds now." I will murder Bernard when I get hold of him.'

It wasn't just American movie stars who descended on Tramp in our first year. We had an eclectic lot, including businessmen and politicians.

One morning the American Embassy rang me and asked if Senator Hubert Humphrey, who challenged Richard Nixon for the presidency, could come to the club with the Attorney-General. I said that that would be fine but, unfortunately, they would have to sit with me.

Humphrey was charm itself. He introduced himself, saying, 'Mr Gold, I've heard so much about you from so many of my fellow countrymen' – which is the usual bullshit line you get from a lot of Americans, but it was nice coming from a man who was nearly President. He and the Attorney-General came and sat with me and we had a stimulating conversation.

But in the corner was Bernie Cornfeld with about five or six ding-a-lings, as was Bernie's wont. You may have forgotten who he was: essentially a playboy who liked lots of women and money. Unfortunately he was later investigated by the American government and it was found that his Investors Overseas Service was in debt to the tune of $600,000,000 – bad news for his investors.

Bernie so far hadn't noticed Senator Humphrey sitting with me, but eventually he did and he came over to the table like a shot from a gun.

'Hubert, how are you?' he said.

'Oh, hi, Bernie,' the senator reluctantly replied.

'What are you doing in town?'

'Well, I'm here with – '

Bernie interrupted him. 'You've got to come over and join me, I've got lots of chicks. Come on over. We'll have some fun.'

Senator Humphrey said, 'I'll see.'

I counted to ten after Bernie left the table. Then Humphrey said to me, 'You know, Mr Gold, I've got a breakfast meeting at five in the morning.'

'Five in the morning?' I repeated.

He got up. 'I'm really sorry, I'm going to have to go. I've really enjoyed it here, though.'

We shook hands but I didn't see him again.

Among our early American members was the singer Harry Nilsson, who was quite a regular at the club. One night he told me he had plugged Tramp in a song and gave me a copy of his new album *Nilsson Schmilsson*. The chorus of the song went, 'So you want me to take you to Tramp? Well, fuck you, fuck you.'

That got played a lot on the radio!

Chapter Twelve

Jackie Collins has written of Tramp, 'Bill Ofner found it, Oscar Lerman designed it and Johnny Gold ran it.'

I think she is being a little too modest. In the early days she and Oscar came down most nights to greet friends and members, many of whom went back to Oscar's Ad Lib days.

Oscar Lerman was a true romantic. He saw a picture of Jackie in a newspaper and determined to marry her, proposing on their first date.

I had known the Collins family ever since I hit London; everybody knew them. The two beautiful sisters, Joan and Jackie, were a forceful presence in the entertainment scene. This was hardly a surprise since their father, Joe, ran a theatrical agency with Lew Grade. Joan, the elder daughter, married a fellow actor, Maxwell Reed, when she was only nineteen. The year she graduated from RADA, she began her film career in *Lady Godiva Rides Again*.

Jackie decided to take a more direct route into movies and ran away from school that same year with the intention of becoming an actress in Hollywood. She stayed with Joan, who had already made her mark as the *femme fatale* in the Howard Hawks film, *Land of the Pharaohs*.

Jackie got parts – usually as the Italian girl with wild hair and body – but was never that burning in her ambition to be an actress. She truly regarded herself as an out-of-work writer rather than an in-work performer. So, at auditions, she would take in the other girls who went along, many of whom were happy to oblige on the casting couch, which was very much in use.

The sisters were close, so much so that when Jackie was pregnant and penniless it was to Joan's husband, Anthony Newley, that she turned for help.

Tony was rich and famous, had been since he played the Artful Dodger in David Lean's *Oliver Twist*. He and Leslie Bricusse had had an enormous hit with *Stop the World – I Want to Get Off* and had an award-winning partnership. They wrote the lyrics for Shirley Bassey's unforgettable Bond song, 'Goldfinger'.

They were a strange pairing from very different backgrounds: Tony came from Hackney and Leslie went to Cambridge. But they sparked each other brilliantly, with Tony the one who liked the limelight. Leslie has a very dry sense of humour. He used to say of another of their collaborations, *The Smell of the Greasepaint – The Roar of the Crowd*, 'We managed to empty every provincial theatre in England.' (Curiously, when Tony took over from Norman Wisdom as the leading character, who was a sort of downcast clown, the show went on to be a Broadway hit.)

There isn't such a thing as a show-business career without severe ups and downs, as I have witnessed more times than I care to remember. Two Oscars on his mantelpiece testify to the fact that Leslie can write. And Tony's standing in Las Vegas was up there, almost on a par with Sinatra and the Rat Pack. However, at the time we opened Tramp he and Joan were promoting a film (written with Herbie Kretzmer, who translated *Les Miserables*) called, I promise you, *Can Hieronymus Merkin Ever Forget Mercy Humppe and Find True Happiness?* It was not the high-point of either Tony's or Joan's career.

Jackie, on the other hand, had discovered she had an eagle eye, an ear like a tape recorder and a commercial gift for writing.

But until she met and married Oscar she was afraid to complete any of her books because she feared they weren't good enough. It was he who encouraged her to take *The World is Full of Married Men*, based on her experiences in LA, to a publisher, and it had become one of the bestsellers of 1969.

People often ask me about the relationship between the Collins sisters. The press like nothing better than to come up with some story showing they detest each other.

But it simply isn't true. Both of them are friends as loyal as any you could wish for. Both are witty, beautiful and tenaciously ambitious. Of course there has been sibling rivalry, but they are different: Joan is never happier than when she is in front of a camera, at work or at play. Jackie would rather be at her desk, sweating out a new novel, and then party at night with friends.

They have shared many experiences together, but they don't live in each other's pocket. Which sisters do? Although usually separated by the Atlantic ocean, they are at each other's side when help is needed. Jackie put it simply to me: 'We are the best of friends and we love each other.'

Jackie has been a host at Tramp, in the UK and LA; Joan would rather be a guest. When Jackie and Oscar moved back to the States, Jackie wrote of the club in her inimitable way: 'It reminds me in the nicest way of a seasoned but friendly and very accommodating old whore. Always there, always ready for your demands and always prepared to give you a good time.'

I was still a single man when the club opened, having broken up, what would turn out to be temporarily, with Jan. Jackie told me I had lost the best woman I would ever know and she was right. So when it came to her knowledge that I was squiring (or dating, as it has now become) other women, she was never slow to remind me of Jan. A very censorious attitude from a woman who has written some of the raciest sex scenes ever committed to print.

One night Ringo asked me, 'What are you doing on Sunday?'

We were closed so I told him the truth: 'Nothing.'

'Right, you're going on a blind date. Meet us in Mr Chow's at nine o'clock.'

My date turned out to be Mia Farrow, the former Mrs Sinatra, who had just had a big hit in Roman Polanski's film, *Rosemary's Baby*. She had a delicate charm that wasn't lost on me.

But, unfortunately, in the same restaurant at the same time was Peter Sellers, who had told me that he was madly in love with Mia. Even worse, André Previn then walked in and his name had been firmly linked with hers (correctly, as it turned out: she had twin sons by him the next year).

You could have cut the atmosphere with a chainsaw. I thought at one stage there was going to be a punch-up and, although I had the training to look after myself, it would hardly have been the best advertisement for the man who was meant to see that everyone had an enjoyable time at Tramp. Although I felt I was in the middle of the War of the Roses, fortunately battle did not break out.

As we left, I whispered to Ringo, 'You certainly know how to fix a guy up with a blind date.'

Jackie was greatly amused by this. I don't think she ever put it in a book – too many other moments in Tramp provided her with ample raw material, such as this:

A Hollywood movie star – male and handsome surveying the room and deciding whose lady he will steal that night; the stately wife of a rich foreign gentleman sending notes to any man she fancied – *and* she usually scored; a major singing stud and a gorgeous beauty queen making out under a table.

'Tramp,' she once wrote, 'has given me more material than I can handle.'

In the first year of the club she wrote her bestseller, *The Stud*, about a millionaire's wife who installs her lover as the manager of her husband's discotheque, a clever move, since it keeps him in check and makes sure that he will satisfy her wishes. He does, however, manage to satisfy one or two other ladies' wishes, as well.

Was it based on me? Well, to a certain extent, maybe. There is something in the nightclub world called 'Rick's Syndrome', named after the club owner Humphrey Bogart played in *Casablanca*. There are some – quite a few, actually – girls who find the man in charge a bit of a challenge because of who he is. So, as a single man, I was quite frequently led into temptation. How often I succumbed to it I will reveal in the sequel to this book!

Jackie, always a punctilious researcher, saw that Rick's Syndrome was not confined to Tramp and based it on a combination of men who ran nightclubs, then spiced the character up with her own fertile imagination.

Oliver Tobias played the title role in what proved to be a very successful film of the book, much of which was shot in Tramp. But the biggest benefactor of the movie was Jackie's big sister as the scheming wife. The part led directly to – and probably inspired – that of Alexis in *Dynasty* which was to make Joan world-famous.

Jackie also had a profound influence on my own life for which I thank her each day.

But I need to turn the clock back a little . . .

The year was 1961 and I had been having a bit of an affair with a girl who was a model. I hadn't seen her for quite a while and she had decided to marry someone else.

She wanted to make quite sure that she had got over me (which came as a shock when I later learnt about it: I never knew she was on me). So, eight days before her wedding, she decided to track me down in a pub called – Jackie would have rejected the name in a novel – the Cock in Great Portland Street, which she knew I frequented every Friday night.

She didn't want to go alone. At the time she was working with Mary Quant's top model, Jan de Souza, and she persuaded her to accompany her.

Jan was reluctant: it had been an exhausting week and all she wanted to do was to get back home to Ealing where she was living with her parents. But she didn't want to let her friend down – which, to this day, is typical of Jan.

The girls came into the Cock and we talked about the wedding and it was apparent to my erstwhile date that I would provide no 'let or hindrance'. But her friend was stunning and blew me away. So I tried chatting her up in my best style.

I always remember, even forty years later, that it was a foggy night, which gave me a great opportunity.

'You can't go back to Ealing. Why don't you stay with me? You can have your own bedroom. You can have a key to the door, don't worry.'

Jan hated me instantly. I was an obnoxious, flash type. They left and I didn't see her again for several months. Then I met her at a party and again I tried my hand and again she didn't want to know.

I suppose it must have been a year later that we met yet again – I was very financially embarrassed at that time (which often happened to me in those days) – and we started to get on very well.

But I was in Brighton and it was difficult for me to come up to town, so nothing happened. Shortly afterwards, I started work at Dollys and Jan used to come to the club with a new American boyfriend, Steve Panama.

She was friendly with a particular group, including Keith Richards of the Stones. In those days Keith didn't smoke, drink, do drugs – he wouldn't even go near a drug (the group comprised Keith Richards, a chap called Roger Shine, Steve Panama and Jan).

Six months later Steve learnt from his firm that he was being sent back to America and he came to me and said, 'Johnny, I want you to do me a favour and look after Jan.'

Right: Jan and David in the south of France.

Below: Tony Newley, me and the babies.
©Joan Collins 1999

Above: Michael, me and the kids.

Below: Robin Williams and Christopher Reeve entertain at my home.

Above: Bond - Roger with my children, Nicky and Claire.

Below: With Peter Sellers circa 1969.

Above: With Prince Andrew at Michael Caine's 4th July party at Langan's.

Above: A normal lunch at the Gold's (left to right): Jan, Nicky, me and Claire.

Right (left to right): Oscar, Jackie, Jan and me.

Left: With Tom Selleck.

Right: A happy man! Between Britt Ekland and Joan Collins.

Left: With Tony Curtis.

Below (left to right): The Tramp Celebrity Cricket Team – Bill Wyman, Errol Brown, Michael Brandon and me.

Above: Jan and I stand proud in Tramp.

Above: With Dodi Fayed at a Cartier polo gathering.

Right : 'The Mayfair Orphans' (left to right): Philip Kingsley, Doug Hayward, Terry O' Neill, Michael Caine, me and Mickey Most.

Below (left to right): me, Mick Jagger, Eric Clapton and Errol Brown.

Above (left to right): Dolph Lundgren towers above John Reid and me.

Right : With Princess Diana and G P Hinduja at the Hinduja home.

Above: With George Best outside Tramp.

Above: Shirley Bassey sings to me, Shakira Caine and Catherine Zeta Jones at Tramp's 30 year anniversary celebration.

Below Left : A shot of Errol and Ginette Brown looking affectionate.

Below Right : With Shirley on the night.

Above: Hollywood highlights (left to right): Joan Collins, Michael Douglas and Catherine Zeta Jones.

Right : With Frankie Dettori.

Above: The glamour girls (left to right): Shirley Bassey, Liz Hurley, Joan Collins and Catherine Zeta Jones.

Above (left to right): me, Tiger Woods, J P McManus, Michael Tabor, Mark O' Meara and Dermot Desmond. © Owen South

I thought: I'd *love* to look after Jan. I fancied her like mad. But I wasn't going to start phoning her as soon as he went away because that would be a naff thing to do. I waited: three months of torture, waiting, and then I phoned her. She said she was coming to the club with some other people and eventually I asked her to come out with me.

That was the beginning.

Eventually we moved in together and lived for about six years in Porchester Place, Bayswater. Then she decided that I was philandering (as if I'd do such a thing!) and she went off to Australia, where she started a new modelling career and a new relationship.

She was away for about two and a half years. During that period of time we opened Tramp. I went out with some nice-looking girls. But none of them were ringing any bells, as Jan had.

Unknown to me, some of our shared friends were conspiring to bring us back together. Shirley Bassey was on a concert tour of Australia. Jan went backstage to see her one evening and Shirley told her, 'You're crazy. There's nobody special in Johnny's life. Go back to London.'

Jackie Collins and even my partner, Oscar, had been writing to Jan all the time, letting her know every move that I was making and every disaster. Evidently they pleaded with Jan to come back so they didn't have to go out with any of my 'ding-a-ling girlfriends' all the time.

Jackie persuaded Jan to come back. At least for a holiday. But I didn't want to be bulldozed and I swore that I didn't want anything to do with her. I told Jackie and Oscar, 'If you want to see her, fine, but I'm not seeing her.'

Then Oscar told me one night, 'We're bringing Jan to the club.'

I was still obdurate: 'Do what you like, but don't sit with me.'

They didn't. They came into the club and sat at the bar – Jackie, Oscar and Jan. I was shocked because she had lost a lot of weight and was very skinny. I hadn't known that the last couple of months she had spent in Australia had not been very happy for her.

We acknowledged each other, but no more than that. However, they kept bringing Jan into the club and gradually we started talking and by Christmas we got back together. We went to the cinema to see *Khartoum* with Charlton Heston as General Gordon. The natives always referred to him as 'Gordon Pasha'. After we came out of the movie Jan pronounced, 'I think we shouldn't go to a restaurant but have supper at home, lasagne and salad.'

I said, 'Yes, Jan Pasha', and I kept calling her Jan Pasha from then on. Eventually it was shortened to Pasha and then Pash, which it remains to this day.

The following February Pash and I went to Tenerife for a holiday to get some sun. I remember saying to her, 'I have to tell you, darling, categorically, I will always love you, but I'm never going to marry you. I just think I have to be fair to tell you that.'

Three months later we got married in Caxton Hall. We didn't really tell anybody. My mother was against the wedding because Jan wasn't Jewish. She was very upset and that hurt me a great deal. So we agreed to make it very low-key: just a few friends at the ceremony and no reception.

I think there were about ten people at our wedding, including Jackie and Oscar, of course, David Millnen, who worked in my racing office, Douggie Hayward the tailor, Jan's parents, Bill Collins (Joan and Jackie's brother), Tricia Guild and Evie Watts, who was a modelling friend of Jan's.

It was one of the last weddings to take place in Caxton Hall. I had phoned to order a car but because I was so intent on keeping it a low-key event I didn't ask for anything special. The firm always used to have really nice cars. But this time a real old banger with an Indian driver turned up at the flat.

I told him, 'I want you to take us to Caxton Hall and then I want you to wait because we're going from Caxton Hall to Heathrow.'

Our guests waited for us on the steps of Caxton Hall. Oscar had a home-movie camera and started filming every Rolls or Daimler that approached, but of course none of them contained us. Then this old banger came along and we stepped out and nobody took the blindest bit of notice.

As you might have gathered, I was more than a little intimidated by marriage and the only thing I remember was Jan's friend, Susie, with her hat all askew, staggering just as Jan was about to say 'I do'. I thought she was going to object in the dramatic way that people do in books and films, but she had a bit of a drinking problem at the time and had gone to the wrong place.

Covered with confetti, Jan and I got back into the battered Ford Cortina and the Indian driver didn't say a word.

Nobody knew our honeymoon destination. We flew to Nice and rented a car to take us to the Voile d'Or hotel on Cap Ferrat. The weather was glorious. We couldn't wait to get into our swimming costumes and head for the pool.

By complete coincidence a member of Tramp who was involved in a club called Sybilla's, Terry Howard, and his girlfriend turned up soon afterwards. Then another friend, David Olivestone.

Strange...

And then George Hamilton arrived with Britt Ekland, who was wearing a wide-brimmed pink hat covered in cherries.

I began to smell a rat – something that was confirmed when Leslie and Evie Bricusse showed up followed by David and Hjourdis Niven.

There must eventually have been more than 25 friends, all ordering bottles of champagne and toasting us and horsing around. I remember that Britt got thrown in the pool. So we had the most marvellous impromptu wedding party.

At the end of the holiday I got the bill and they had to give me mouth-to-mouth resuscitation – every bottle and all the orders were on my bill. I thought I was going to have to take out a mortgage to pay it – but it was worth every franc.

Back at Tramp life became somewhat changed. Jan had no desire to spend every evening in the apartment on her own so she joined me at Tramp nearly every night.

She knew many of the members from her days at Dollys and soon got to know the rest: the art of running a club is to be able to greet every member by name and make introductions when you think it appropriate – or even romantic.

Jan was not without admirers in her own right and young men were often eager to spend time at her table. She was a regular at the club for twenty years or more where she was a tremendous asset, helping to entertain our guests. I could never express what she means to me – she is without a doubt the most chic, beautiful woman ever who has also raised two fabulous kids, put up with my hours and charmed all those who have come into contact with her. She's the love of my life.

Thus the pressures of Rick's Syndrome were to abate considerably. Since we had kept things quiet about our marriage – or thought we had! – one or two young women used occasionally to come across to see how I was getting on. Jackie was nearly always on hand, a smiling bulldog, to introduce them to Mrs Gold.

But, sometimes, on my own, I was made an offer I could refuse. For instance, one evening a girl I had never seen before came into the club – Brigitte Bardot-ish – with long blonde hair. She was with another girl, whom I didn't know either. I was sitting at my table and, sometime during the course of the evening, the two girls came over to the table; one of them seemed to know somebody with me. They sat down and joined us.

The Bardot blonde, who had a very bare midriff, started to talk to me, then went away to dance but later came back and leant forward and said, 'Would you like to have sex with me?'

I replied, 'That's a very sporting offer, but why would you want to have sex with an old fart like me? How old are *you?*'

'Twenty-three.'

'Why would you want to have sex with me?'

She leant closer. 'I'm a nymphomaniac.'

I said, 'I suppose it's better than being a kleptomaniac.'

'Will you take me shopping afterwards?' she asked.

I said I didn't think any shops were open at night.

'No, during the day.'

I asked where she'd like to go shopping and she said she loved Harvey Nichols.

I replied, 'The place I really like shopping is Marks & Spencer, so that will have to do.'

I never saw her again.

Pash was once asked by a journalist how she felt about me being surrounded by a bevy of dingalings. 'I just put a sheep dip outside the bedroom door as a sanitation measure, for Johnny to go through!' was her response.

Chapter Thirteen

I determined that there should be no dress code at Tramp. People would come in sneakers, blue jeans and T-shirts and sit down next to people in full evening dress. The sixties had imposed a new order on what people wore. Nobody cared. The only thing I didn't like was shorts for men. On hot summer nights I didn't stop them coming in but I would suggest they wear long trousers the next time.

Over the years I've noticed how much smarter people's dress has become than it ever used to be. The youngsters of today are very much more into suits than they ever were in the sixties. In the sixties no one wanted to wear a suit and tie; the scruffy look was in. But today more and more of the kids like wearing suits. You see all the ads for youngsters' clothing now, and the girls are much prettier and more smartly dressed, and that is much more today's style. They are all very conscious of what's in, what's fashionable.

Dance styles have changed, too. I remember when I first opened Tramp, and certainly in Dollys, if I saw girls dancing together, I would ask them to get off the floor, because that was real dancehall stuff – shocking, dancing round your handbags. But today it's very common. A lot of girls dance together and a lot of guys dance together, too.

In the sixties there was this dance called the Madison and we all had little teams of dancers. There were certain steps that you followed. You always hoped that your team was better than the other team and that was the beginning of dancing in a group, whereas today I see it happen all the time. Ten people are having dinner and the whole table get up and have a dance.

Now it's nearly always a girl who takes a guy to dance! It's far less the norm to see the guy asking the girl – unless he's gone over to try to pick up a girl he wasn't with.

They say a convoy is as fast as its slowest ship and, in many ways, a club is as good as the hands-on staff. Whether it is the sous-chefs or the trainee waiters who clear the tables or the girls at reception, speed, efficiency, politeness and a positive attitude and cheerful mien make the difference between a happy ship and a sinking one.

Guido has been with me from the absolute beginning. He started as the assistant manager. Our first manager was a man called Louis who was Spanish. He was extremely good but always wanted to do everything himself and would run around the club like a crazy person. Guido, in contrast, was very quiet, retiring and shy, and didn't seem to have much personality at all. He left after about eighteen months – I've never asked him where he went to. But after about two years, he came back. Louis had left and we made him manager.

Now he has been at the helm for nearly thirty years. He could have been a brilliant Italian politician, such is his discretion in handling the demands of the famous and those who think they are famous. He can deal tactfully with every booking to make the person on the other end of the line think they are *the* most important member, greet them and their guests as if they were royalty (sometimes they are) and guide them to their favourite table.

Guido's personality now knows no bounds: he's very outgoing, all the customers know and like him. He's wonderful because he

speaks many languages and he really knows how I think after all
these years. I have no qualms if I'm not there, because I know
that he'll handle things correctly. He also has his able
lieutenants: Damir who controls the disco with utmost cool and
Dario, in the restaurant, somehow squeezing ten people around a
table of eight without anyone complaining. His newest, John
Brown, who hails from Tasmania, is great too.

Part of my ritual is to phone the club at 8.30 p.m. to go
through the reservations and make certain that nobody has crept
in who shouldn't be there. I also make sure that everybody in the
club is aware that I'm checking up.

People have their favourite tables. A lot of people think the
tables at the back of the restaurant by the fireplace are bad
tables. But they don't necessarily know that Robert De Niro
loves sitting there and so does the Sultan of Brunei.

Some people set a lot of store by where they sit in a room and
they get really uptight. It doesn't happen so much in clubs but I
see it happening in restaurants. They're upset if they're not in *the*
area to sit in, *the* section to be acknowledged in. It's almost, if you
like, a salute to their achievements that they are allowed to sit in
certain places in a club or restaurant. I think this is utter bullshit,
but it's how it is. I've seen people going into a restaurant – maybe
the upstairs is the place to sit – and, if they can't go upstairs, they
won't sit downstairs because it's beneath them.

It's like stars in Hollywood. If they've made a reservation and
they arrive and their table's not ready, they won't hang around
because it's almost like an insult to their standing. It shows that
they might be slipping and they don't want to lose face waiting
at the bar when there might be film producers or directors sitting
there noting that they can't get a table.

In the beginning Bill Ofner was the wine and food man. He
had learnt the art of doing a clever deal from his days at the
Society. For instance, he pointed out to Paul Krug how, if Krug
was to be our house champagne, then our members would also

order it elsewhere and probably buy a few crates for their cellars. Krug saw the logic in this and we were able to purchase our supplies cheaper than anyone else in London.

Bill was an amazing character. He had actually been to school with Pope John Paul II in Poland. Their lives went separate ways: Bill was managing a band on tour in Russia when the Germans invaded his native country and he never went back, or else he would have become a certain victim of the Holocaust.

Instead he came to England, joined the British army and was awarded the Military Cross for gallantry. He used to look after the finances and was, as I've mentioned, financially cautious. The electrics would go wrong or things would break down but Bill, bless him, never wanted to spend a penny on anything. He would always try to make do with second-hand equipment. You could have a Hoover that would break down nine times and we'd keep having it repaired instead of buying a new one. It would usually end up costing us more money.

But he was a genius in his own right. He spoke seven languages fluently, he was as good as any accountant you could ever wish to get and almost as good as any lawyer.

All his life he was a very heavy smoker of serious cigarettes: Senior Service untipped. In 1986 he got a thrombosis in his leg and was rushed to the Middlesex Hospital. I went to see him just moments after the doctors had told him that they would have to amputate his leg. He was white. He couldn't bear the thought of it.

So we contacted his cousin, who was a doctor in America. He used his contacts and tracked down two English surgeons who managed to save his leg, although he went through a year of hell. During this time Bill's live-in lover, Maggie Sarnagne, was constantly by his bedside. She was a stunning French singer who toured the world – including Vegas – and also sang at the Society when it was still going.

During Bill's illness I took over ordering the wines and food, costing the budget and looking for deals with merchants, something which I enjoyed.

Bill and I had decided on the menu, which stayed virtually the same for many years. Starters were asparagus with smoked salmon, jumbo prawns and Parma ham and melon. The favoured main courses were grilled sole (the biggest you could get), baby poussin, big steaks and especially hamburgers. It was all Oscar's idea to have 'zodiac hamburgers' because the ceiling had a zodiac circle and all around the restaurant wall there are the zodiac signs. So we offered twelve different burgers, one for each sign of the zodiac. For instance, the Cancer Burger was a bacon burger.

One of the favourite dishes was bangers and mash. In the kitchen Willie, our chef for thirty years, arranged the dish into a phallic symbol. Willie had a habit of cutting messages out of cheese and putting them on top of this. If a man arrived at dinner in a bad mood and then found 'Have you had it up lately?' written on his meal, the effect was miraculous. Equally few girls could forebear to smile if 'Are you feeling sexy?' was emblazoned on their dinner.

Sometimes messages were individualised. 'Is your man still good?' was written on Jack Nicholson's sausage the day his movie, *A Few Good Men*, premiered. 'Good for a Shaft?' he put on Sidney Poitier's plate, which didn't greatly amuse him because the star of *Shaft* was actually Richard Roundtree.

Unfortunately, there was an underground lake beneath the club, which tended to rise after a prolonged rainy season. We had to put in sump pumps to drain out the water. But it still sometimes used to get through. We used to have to put down duckboards and cardboard boxes.

I can remember the night that Roger Moore and Tony Curtis, who were appearing together in *The Persuaders*, were having an early dinner in the restaurant. The flood waters started to seep in and they were down on their hands and knees with the staff trying to stem them.

Members would come squelching in and look in some surprise at these two. But dinner service went on with the women being lifted up to get to the tables. It was hysterical.

I was worried, though, that we might be caught by the health inspector. There was one particularly officious health officer who was always trying to get us closed down. He took us to the magistrates but we managed to obtain what they call a protection order, which means you can continue operating without getting your licence. Then we went to court proper and we won. Basically he wanted to make a name for himself as the man who closed Tramp.

However, we did lose our drinking licence for a week. Behind Tramp there used to be another club called the Pigalle. At that time there was a combined licence for the two premises because in the old days the Society and the Pigalle were owned by the same company. The premises never reverted to separate licences or even to separate ratings. It was all done as one.

There was a bit of a row at Tramp one night when a rich Iranian guy, who wasn't a member, tried to get into the club. He became really furious and said, 'I'm going to buy these places and throw you out.'

He was as good – or as bad – as his word. He bought the Pigalle (which he and his partners turned into Xenon on Piccadilly) and thus became our landlord. And he tried to get rid of us.

But Bill was far too smart for him and he failed miserably. However, the guy later forgot to renew the licence. So one day the police phoned and informed us our licence had not been renewed.

I promised to do so straightaway but they told me it was too late. I was astounded. 'What do you mean – too late?'

The police insisted: 'You can't get it renewed for a week until the magistrate sits again.'

I said, 'Are you telling me that I can't serve any alcohol?'
'You certainly can't.'

I couldn't believe it. I was choked when I told Bill we were unlicensed premises but he, ever the lawyer, established that people could bring their own booze – as many 'BYOB' restaurants do in Melbourne – but we couldn't charge corkage.

So, when people rang up to make reservations for dinner, they were told, 'I'm sorry, you'll have to bring your own booze because we haven't got a licence for a week.'

It was a wild situation. We lost money that week but it was probably one of the most memorable weeks of Tramp, with people coming down with cases of alcohol.

There would be, say, ten people for dinner. They would bring a whole lot of booze. Then people would arrive later on for a drink or to dance who didn't know we didn't have a licence. So the other people would offer them drinks.

It became one huge private party in there every night and the customers had an absolute ball. I loved it.

And the guy who bought Xenon went bust.

Subsequently we lived through the three-day week, courtesy of Mr Edward Heath in the winter of 1974. We had a power-cut at about eleven o'clock every night. Everything went off, except the gas in the kitchen, so we could still cook. But the music stopped and the lights went out. The club was illuminated by candles and torches. At about 1 a.m. the place was full and everyone was sitting, talking. I started singing songs and people joined in and there was a terrific wartime spirit.

Then suddenly the lights burst on and the music came back on at the same time. Boom! The whole place exploded. They jumped up in the air, hugging, dancing, dancing on the tables, everywhere. We had these nights of sheer joy with people having more fun than ever.

It was amazing. Out of all these disasters, there's always a funny side to things. Great days.

Chapter Fourteen

Romance often reared its irresistible head in Tramp – even for the stars.

Tom Selleck was an early member and a regular whenever he was in London. I really liked and admired him. He was six foot four and a terrific athlete – in fact he had gone to the University of Southern California on an athletic scholarship.

He told me, and I believed him, 'I was planning to go into architecture. But, when I tried to sign up for it, the class was full. Acting was right next to it. So I signed up for acting, instead.'

With his craggy handsome face he was a natural for the big screen, although he used to hang his head in shame when he recalled his dreadful debut film: *Myra Breckenridge*, a camp attempt to reinstall Mae West as a film star after 26 years. It didn't.

Nor did it open many movie doors for Tom, who was to make his name on television playing the title role in *Magnum, P.I.* – a laid-back private dick in a Hawaiian shirt. It made him a very recognisable figure but he shrugged his shoulders as he related how no sooner had the ink dried on his contract than Steven Spielberg offered him the lead in *Raiders of the Lost Ark* – a role that has helped Harrison Ford on his way to billionaire status. Tom was philosophical about it – a nice guy and a good sport.

One night he arrived at the club having just seen Andrew Lloyd Webber's *Cats*. He collapsed on a chair at my table.

'Johnny, I need a drink!'

'That bad?' I asked. 'I rather liked it.'

'Me, too. But I've seen this girl. I'm in love.'

I asked what she looked like and he said he didn't know because she wore a mask. A few days later he went to see the show again. And again he came back to Tramp.

'Oh, this girl is so great, Johnny. She's fantastic, incredible, she's wonderful.'

When he went to the show for the third time he persuaded Brian Blessed, who was the first Old Deuteronomy, to take him backstage to meet her.

That night Tom brought her to the club. She was called Jillie Mack, a bit like Annie Hall wearing antique, second-hand clothes.

She was bubbly and proved to be totally outrageous, always making tongue-in-cheek sexual innuendoes. I can remember her sitting with Joan Collins and Alana Stewart, discussing sizes of boobs. She was always trying to shock or embarrass me. At the time of writing, she's been married to Tom for fourteen years and they have a little daughter, Hannah.

And then there was my dear friend Michael Caine – Sir Michael. After his divorce from Patricia, whom he married when he was 22, he became a born-again bachelor, sharing a pad with Terence Stamp.

Michael had a solid British film career that went ballistic with *Alfie* in 1966. An American friend of Oscar's and later a regular at our Friday-night table, Mike Baumohl, worked closely with the director, Lewis Gilbert, on that picture. First, they filled it with well-known names: Millicent Martin, Jane Asher, Julia Foster, Eleanor Bron, Vivien Merchant (wife of Harold Pinter) and, significantly, an American star, Shelley Winters.

When it was finished, Paramount didn't even want to release

it. Certainly not in America, where they said they would have to revoice Michael if they did.

But Mike Baumohl, an ace publicist, showed it individually to top critics: Peter Evans, Alexander Walker and Chuck Champlin of *Time* magazine. They loved it. Michael Caine revoiced a few lines and the rest is history: a £350,000 production made more than £10 million and Michael was nominated for an Oscar. He became an international Superstar and screen legend. But it didn't go to his head and he didn't forget his old friends, as I've witnessed in other cases.

Although a regular at the Ad Lib and Dollys and a founder member of Tramp, Michael would spend many of his evenings in his Grosvenor Square flat on his own reading, a passion since childhood. He became an erudite, self-taught man. He used to leave the TV on with the sound down. One night he glanced up and saw an advertisement for Maxwell House coffee set in Brazil with the most beautiful woman he had ever set eyes on.

He could no longer concentrate on his book, so he grabbed a cab, arrived in Tramp and told me he was going to Brazil the following day to track down this fabulous vision.

In walked Nigel Pollitzer, always known for some reason as 'the Rat'. Michael told him of his experience and Nigel said there was no need for him to go to Brazil.

'Why not?' demanded Michael.

'Because she lives in South Kensington.'

She was Shakira Baksh, who had come third in the 1967 Miss World contest and consequently arrived in England to try to make it in films. She played a native girl in *Carry On Doctor* with Frankie Howerd and Barbara Windsor.

The Rat was even able to give Michael Shakira's agent's telephone number. He took her to dinner the following night and for the past twenty-nine years she has been Mrs, now Lady, Caine.

It's among the things in my life that have given me great satisfaction: playing a small part in helping Michael, whom I adore, find the wife who was waiting for him, whom I also adore. Shakira and Jan are great pals and the four of us have had some truly memorable times together.

I've known Bill Wyman since 1964: he, like the other Stones and Beatles, used to come to Dollys with various women. Then, he was quiet and shy compared with the others.

We became really close mates when he came back to London after living in France. He was a born-again bachelor, too, and a regular at Tramp. I always thought he must have been a surgeon in another life. A slow and meticulous eater, he would delicately dissect a T-bone steak or neatly cut the white off a fried egg, leaving an unbroken yolk. It was amazing to watch – and was evidently not restricted to his eating. Some girl he went with told the *News of the World* of her experiences with him for a few quid, revealing he had been a wonderful lover with such nimble fingers. So I always used to call him 'Nimble' – something he has never complained about!

What he did complain about was my support of Brighton and Hove Albion, since he was passionate – well, as passionate as you can be – about Crystal Palace and for years they were in the same division.

We had a common passion in cricket. Bill was a member of a side I put together for a charity tournament, along with Adam Faith, Errol Brown, Michael Brandon and – if you're going to have a ringer choose the best – Imran Khan. Bill got quite keen on charity cricket after that.

We used to play his 1982 hit 'Si, Si, Je Suis Un Rock Star' a lot at Tramp. It was the biggest solo chart hit for any of the Stones. He enjoyed the single life and would sometimes arrive accompanied by two or three girls. But on an icy February night in 1984 he arrived with just one. Mandy Smith.

Bill, then 48, had always preferred younger women and

Mandy, a pretty blonde, looked about eighteen or nineteen. I was amazed when he confided that she was only thirteen. My first reaction was to say that she could not be served any alcohol – not that she wanted any.

Bill had met her at some music awards. And, quite simply, he fell in love with her. The press had a field day when they found out.

That spring Jan and I were in the South of France staying at the Colombe d'Or. Bill had a home up in Vence and went there once the news about him and Mandy broke. He couldn't go out because he was permanently besieged by the press and photographers.

We would smuggle him out at night in the back of our car. Bill later wrote in the *Independent on Sunday* (2 May 2000): 'Johnny was the only person who helped me through that stressful time; all my other friends went blank on me.'

I collected him on his own late one night. Bill had to slip into the back of my car and, as usual, cover himself with a beach towel to get past the mob.

We went back to the Colombe d'Or, where we met up with James Baldwin (the gay American writer and poet). James also had a house in St Paul de Vence. The three of us sat in the bar, recounting stories and jokes and exchanging profundities but mainly getting more and more drunk. But Baldwin, who loved his whisky, got more drunk than we knew: he began to talk in slow motion, then fell flat on the floor. For a moment we thought he had died – how the press would have enjoyed that. But he was merely unconscious. We had to carry him back to his house, where we put him to bed. He was fine the next day.

Contrary to most people's expectations, Bill's relationship with Mandy lasted and he married her when she was eighteen. They held a great party at the Dorchester to celebrate, and when someone took that photo of me, Mick Jagger, Eric Clapton and Errol Brown, Mick was expressing a genuine worry over whether the marriage would last the long tour the Stones were about to embark on. It didn't. Mandy suffered from an eating disorder and they broke up after less than two years.

In 1993 Bill left the Rolling Stones. He told me he didn't want to be a grandfather rock-and-roller and I think he was absolutely right.

Bill is a great collector. He has a metal detector and goes round the beaches. When you go to his house at Bledding, it's like a museum. There are glass cabinets full of Roman remains, ancient arrows and artefacts, stuff he's found on beaches with his metal detector. He loves archaeology and all his findings are meticulously labelled and annotated by date.

Today Bill is married again to Suzanne – a fabulous American woman; they now have three beautiful daughters – and he honoured Jan and me by asking us to be godparents to their youngest child, Matilda, better known as Matty.

Although in different groups, Bill and Ringo were drawn to each other. They both had a certain outsider quality and also a quiet, dry humour for those who would listen. They even started a restaurant, the Brassier, in Atlanta, Georgia, but it wasn't a success – unlike Sticky Fingers, Bill's hamburger ventures, which were Aladdin's caves of Stones memorabilia. When Mick Jagger signed a multimillion-dollar contract for his memoirs, he realised he had not kept any diaries or records, so he went to Bill to see if he would provide him with them. But Bill declined with, shall we say, a brief and forthright Anglo-Saxon saying, as he was writing his own book.

Ringo – Ritchie to his friends – had been a regular at Dollys with Maureen, his wife. I introduced him to another member, Hilary Gerard, a very strait-laced stockbroker and an old friend. The two men got on so well that Hilary gave up the City to become Ringo's financial adviser. Over the years his black jacket and striped trousers turned to T-shirt and jeans and, for a while, the Indian cult garb of the Beatles' seventies days. He became part of Ringo's family, which he is to this day.

Ringo was always drawn to acting. He had been the most sympathetic Beatle in *A Hard Day's Night* and, after the group broke up, went on to give another lovely performance in *That'll Be The Day*. His own production, *Son of Dracula*, which he starred in with his great mate, Harry Nilsson, was seen by very few of us and the very few of us who saw it can understand why.

That the Beatles ceased to function as a group didn't mean they discontinued their friendships. All the other three contributed tracks to Ringo's hit album *Ringo* in 1973 – the year that he bought Tittenhurst Park from John Lennon. I asked him what he was going to do with a 25-room mansion and he replied, 'Build on to it.'

But soon after he moved there his marriage to Maureen began to break up. He became yet another born-again bachelor, back at Tramp with a variety of dates and quite an appetite for a good time.

I thought he was going to marry an American girl, Nancy Andrews, with whom he lived in Monte Carlo (so did she: she got Marvin Mitchelson to sue him for palimony after they split up). But it was another American who finally curtailed his single days and ways.

Barbara Bach made an enormous impact playing opposite Roger Moore in *The Spy Who Loved Me*. She wasn't just another Bond girl: she was the imperious Major Anya Amasova, Soviet Agent XXX. The sight of her in scanty clothes tied to a sofa by evil Curt Jurgens was one that, for some reason, stays in the memory.

Ringo met her properly when they were both cast in *Caveman*, a comedy written and directed by Carl Gottlieb, who co-wrote the screenplay for *Jaws*. The location was in Mexico, where, he confessed, it was pretty well love at first sight. When filming finished they were inseparable, except by a nasty car crash in May 1980 that nearly did for them both.

But they were back at Tramp by the end of the summer,

drinking and smoking (something they would never do in their reformed life today). Ringo was also back working with Paul on an album. He told me in the strictest confidence one evening that he and Barbara were going to get married in the new year and asked if he could use my restaurant, Rags, for the reception. I gave him a huge hug of congratulation and told him it would be a privilege.

But on 8 December that year John Lennon was murdered and the first people to fly to New York to comfort Yoko Ono were Ringo and Barbara. They knew it was inappropriate for them to marry in what proved to be a period of worldwide mourning, so the ceremony was postponed.

Rags, incidentally, was just off Curzon Street in the West End. The idea had been to create a daytime place for Tramp members to go at lunchtime and also to attract people from other walks of life who might not be Tramp members. In retrospect that was a mistake. What we should have done was make the Tramp members become Rags members – if we'd done that, Rags would probably be going strong today.

In the early days it had been a lot of fun. It attracted people from the music industry because a lot of the music industry were all around there – Charles Street and Mayfair. They've all since moved. But there were nights when Dudley Moore would go and play the piano – and Alan Price from the Animals used to come and play and sing.

However, its finest hour was 27 April 1981. After their marriage at Marylebone Town Hall, Barbara and Ringo and her two children (by her previous marriage to an Italian businessman – Francesca, 12, and Gianni, 8) and his three children from his marriage to Maureen (Zak, 15, Jason, 12, and Lee, 10) and Paul and Linda McCartney and George and Olivia Harrison and seventy other friends followed by about seven hundred fans descended on Rags for lunch.

BEATLEMANIA IS BACK was the front-page headline on the next day's *Sun*, covered in photos of the Fab Three.

We had shrimp and salmon and beef for lunch and nobody enjoyed it more than Ringo's mother, Elsie, who came down from Liverpool. Barbara's father, Howard, was also over from New York. Her mother, Susan, had recently remarried Georgie Peckham, the guitarist of the Mersey group, the Fourmost.

When enough champagne had gone down, somebody produced guitars and drums and the three Beatles played together in public for the first time in ten years. It was just chilling to hear them sing 'All My Loving' as fresh as if it had just been written.

I was proud that the reunion took place in my restaurant, a pride tinged with the sadness that the Fab Four would never all be together again.

Chapter Fifteen

Just as the privacy of Tramp made it a safe haven for stars, so it did for members of royal families, British and foreign. In fact, most royals used to be a great deal more relaxed about coming to the club than some celebrities. Whereas a British prince would have a lone detective sipping a soda at a corner table, the singer formerly known as Prince arrived with six.

I have already written how, in their early days, Princess Margaret and Lord Snowdon would cavort about the place with Peter Sellers. After their marriage in 1960 they were fairly focal in the London scene: dinner at San Lorenzo and then on to Tramp. Margaret loved to dance. I remember her complaining bitterly: 'John, you must talk to that husband of mine: I want to dance.'

They were lovely times, those days. Margaret liked her Famous Grouse malt whisky with Malvern water; Tony liked his red wine; and both smoked like chimneys. After their divorce in 1978, they didn't come individually but by the 1980s their children did. Viscount Linley was very much a regular and Lady Sarah Armstrong-Jones came along with parties of friends.

They were exceptionally polite and very down to earth – a credit to their parents. I remember Viscount Linley coming from the Abbey after Andrew and Sarah's wedding and I said, 'You must be shattered,' and he said: 'I am, but I just needed to unwind' – which was exactly the purpose of the club.

Princess Anne, sweet nineteen and fresh from her school Benenden, in Kent, was a furious dancer. She had a great sense of humour. One Saturday night I asked her what she was doing the next day and she said she was going to the Remembrance Day ceremony at the Cenotaph. I said it must be a very solemn occasion and she agreed, but admitted she always had the desire when standing on the balcony to hold up a big sign saying, HELLO FOLKS!

I offered her the use of the back door if she wanted to make an exit with an escort – even in the early days a few paparazzi stalked the entrance – but she always said, 'I don't mind.'

Prince Michael of Kent was a regular, distinctively suited and booted with a beard that makes him look like George V. Usually he was with a group of friends but sometimes he would just come for a drink on his own. He always liked to sit at the same table.

Nigel Pollitzer – the 'Rat' – usually came to the club with a group of friends headed up by Paddy MacNally, a man who had made a mint out of Formula One motor racing. Paddy was, and is, a very generous man and an old friend.

Then he started to go out with Sarah Ferguson. She loved to dance, but sometimes seemed a bit outnumbered by the MacNally set. Sarah (I never called her Fergie – that nickname came along afterwards) used to come and sit with me and share a cigarette and let them get on with it. That way we became friendly. I think she was working for Harrods at the time, in the marketing department.

I loved her company: a real people person with such a zest for life. She introduced me to her father, Major Ronald Ferguson, a former Life Guards officer, and I became quite friendly with him, too. He used to come down to the club – always had an eye for a pretty girl.

I thought that Sarah and Paddy would always remain friends, even after they broke up, and happily that proved to be the case.

Prince Andrew at the time was dating Koo Stark, the daughter of an American film producer. They, too, came to Tramp, but were at great pains to make sure the press had minimal information about their relationship. Maybe because it was more fragile than anyone realised.

One Tuesday Prince Andrew came to see me and told me a certain unnamed redhead had asked him to give me a hug. It was before there was anything in the papers about their relationship. Andrew wanted to book a party for Thursday for his captain and fellow officers and wives and girlfriends to have a celebratory dinner. He doesn't drink alcohol but he sat with me until two in the morning, just the two of us chattering away with cups of tea.

When it came time for him to leave I asked Guido, 'Is His Royal Highness's car here?'

He said, 'The car's here, but there's some paparazzi outside.'

We suggested he might want to leave by a back exit but Andrew wasn't worried. 'Johnny, it doesn't matter at all because I'm by myself, I'm not doing any harm. It's nothing.'

As he left the club, I said, 'Goodbye and see you soon.'

The day after that, the *Sun* headline was, PRINCE ANDREW BOOGIES THE NIGHT AWAY WITH KOO STARK – with a photo of him outside Tramp. It went on: 'Fellow club members said they only had eyes for one another and danced really romantically. At 2.00 a.m. Prince Andrew left by the front door and Koo left by the back door. Andrew met her later at her apartment.'

Koo was nowhere near the club that night. The whole thing was a total fabrication. Yet people believe what they read in the newspapers. Why should facts spoil a good story?

Andrew used to come fairly frequently to Tramp. One night he was in with some friends, including Charlie Young (an old school chum who was often with him). Michael Caine and Roger Moore were there that night and so were the Bee Gees and Rod Stewart. Andrew leant across to me (he was sitting at another table, just across the aisle) and he said, 'Johnny, isn't it great, all these famous people in here!'

Minutes later, one of the Bee Gees, Maurice Gibb, asked me, 'Is there any chance we could meet Prince Andrew, Johnny?'

I said that I could probably arrange it. So I went over to Andrew and I said, 'I'm really sorry to bother you, if you don't want to it doesn't matter at all, but the Bee Gees would really like to meet you.'

He was most keen. 'Oh, I'd like to meet them, Johnny, that would be great.'

I said, 'Well, I'll do it very informally, we'll just walk by the table and, if I may, I'll just introduce you.'

So I told Maurice, 'Yes, His Royal Highness would like to meet you. What we'll do is this: you go out to the toilet and then, when you come back, I'll come back in with you and we'll stop by the table and I'll introduce you.'

They wanted to smarten themselves up a bit, so I took them up to my office and they inspected themselves in the mirrors, had a wash and made sure their hair was correct.

When we came back downstairs, we stopped and I said, 'Excuse me, Your Royal Highness, may I introduce Maurice and Barry Gibb?' They had quite a long chat together and off they went, extremely thankful and content.

It remains my belief that, no matter how friendly you may or may not be, there's always a certain protocol with members of the royal family. Although I was closely acquainted with Andrew and we would sit and chat for a long time together, at the beginning of the evening, when I first saw him, I would always say, 'Good evening, Your Royal Highness,' and then later, during the course of the evening, I would call him Andrew.

One particular night, when Jan and I were having dinner in Tramp with Prince Andrew and Sarah and Michael and Shakira Caine, Kirk Douglas walked in, with his wife Anne and his youngest son, Eric. They stopped at the table and I stood up. Kirk went round the table, gave Shakira a kiss, Michael a hug and then me a hug. I introduced Kirk to Andrew who was now standing and was obviously pleased to see Kirk Douglas. It was Kirk's 71st birthday.

But Anne Douglas was busy talking to Shakira Caine. Now the protocol is: you don't keep a member of the royal family standing while you're busy gossiping. It just doesn't happen. Anne is, of course, very socially accepted – they call her 'the Queen of Hollywood'.

But Andrew in the end got fed up standing and sat down. I could see exactly what was happening – he had started a deep conversation with Sarah. Anne Douglas then came round the table. I stood up and gave her a kiss but I could see there was no way I could introduce her. You don't tap royalty on the shoulder, nor do you interrupt them. So I didn't introduce them.

The Douglases went and sat at the top table in the restaurant and I thought to myself: When they finish their meal, I'll then introduce Anne to Andrew on the way out. But when they left, Anne shot right past our table without a by-your-leave or a goodbye to anybody. Kirk stopped and said goodbye and their son stopped and then off they went. I was very friendly with Anne and Kirk. Anne always used to say, 'Thank you for keeping an eye on my boys' – her sons and stepsons.

About an hour later, the phone rang and it was Eric Douglas demanding to speak to me. 'How could you do that to my mother?' he yelled. 'How could you insult her that way?'

'What on earth are you talking about?' I asked.

'How could you not introduce her to the Prince?'

I said, 'Now listen, you know I would have introduced her but there is protocol and I have to abide by the protocol. Now I know how important Anne is in Hollywood and I love and adore her and you don't think I would do anything like that?'

I went on to explain the whole situation, but he insisted: 'Well, I think you should send flowers to apologise.'

I told him, 'I'm not going to send flowers to apologise because I wasn't the one who behaved incorrectly. When you're in England and it's a member of our royal family, you have to act accordingly. I don't know how you act towards the President of the USA or the First Lady or whoever it is, but here there's a protocol and Anne happened to break that protocol. You don't leave a member of the royal family standing there like a lemon while she's busy gossiping. I'm really sorry, but you can tell her from me that I did not in any way mean to insult her – I was going to introduce her when she left, but she left in such a huff I didn't have a chance to!'

And there the matter rested.

On 23 July 1986 Jan and I went to Andrew and Sarah's wedding. The night before, they had a wonderful party. We sat with Michael and Shakira and David and Carina Frost. There were three marquees and our table was right on the dance floor. Andrew and Sarah started the dancing and when they got to our table, Andrew said, 'Johnny, come and dance!'

I stood up immediately and said, 'Come on, Jan.'

We would be the only other couple on the dance floor so, quite reasonably, she refused. 'No, I'm not getting up.'

I said, 'Darling, I think we have to.'

Michael Caine chipped in: 'Go on, you've got to do it. You heard what he said, it's a royal command.'

So we stood up and took to the floor. I saw that a couple of other people were dancing now, so it was all right. I whispered, 'Pash, don't look now, but we're the only commoners on this dance floor. Look, the Queen's dancing with Ronnie Ferguson, the Queen Mum's dancing with Viscount Linley.' Princess Margaret was dancing with a foreign royal and so was Princess Anne. The whole family was on the dance floor. Nancy Reagan was dancing with Prince Charles. I know she and Major Ferguson aren't quite royals – but you know what I mean.

Sarah and Andrew seemed such a natural couple, very much

suited to each other with their open sense of humour and active sporting lives. They used to come to the club a lot after they were married. I remember eating dinner with them when Sarah was pregnant with her first daughter. I was really sad when their marriage went wrong for them. I think that if he hadn't been in the navy and she had not been left to her own devices for so long, perhaps it wouldn't have happened. It was that long time apart. She was newly married and he was away for six months, which is tough on any girl. I guess it was just too tough for her.

Sarah later came to Tramp with her new beau, John Bryant. I didn't greatly care for him. Neither did her father, who said to me one night, 'Johnny, can't you get her away from this awful Bryant fellow.'

I pointed out that separating couples was not part of my remit. Byant used to hang on the coat-tails of Steve Wyatt and seemed to be anxious for as much publicity as possible. But, when it came, it was of the wrong kind.

I've always liked Sarah. She's made a lot of mistakes along the way. She knows she's made mistakes, we talked about them the last time I saw her. There she was, a girl in terrible financial difficulties, and she pushed herself along, albeit on the back of the royal family, but she made a big success of herself in America to get herself out of debt. I doff my hat to her because she's done it.

One night in the winter of 1971 two well-dressed gentlemen arrived at the desk in Jermyn Street. The receptionist phoned down and said, 'There's a Crown Prince of Sweden upstairs, says he's Carl Gustaf.'

I had no idea what Carl Gustaf looked like so I asked some friends and senior staff if anyone else did. Nobody had any idea. So I telephoned back upstairs: 'Tell him to go away. He might be a smorgasbord salesman as far as I'm concerned, I wouldn't know the difference.'

Needless to say, the following day I had the Swedish Embassy on the phone explaining that the Crown Prince had come to the club the previous night and he had very much wanted to come in.

I pointed out to them: 'If somebody had phoned me from the embassy to warn me about it, I would have arranged his entry for him.'

The First Secretary then asked whether Carl Gustaf could become a member. I told him I thought we might be able to fix that and he replied, 'Well, actually, he's coming tonight with a member.'

Which he did. The member introduced him to me and I found him absolutely charming. The Prince told me he would like to become a member. His friend proposed him, we found another member to second him and thus the rules were observed.

Carl came to the club many times while he was the Crown Prince. His father had died in an air crash when he was only one. So when his grandfather – the interim monarch – died in 1973 Carl became King.

He still came to the club, but far less frequently. One evening he arrived with a German girl, Silvia Sommerlath, to whom he had become engaged. He told me how they had met at the 1972 Munich Olympics, where she had been working. They seemed very much in love.

The next time I saw them they were married and Silvia was Queen of Sweden. They now arrived with security with them and a couple of friends. They seemed to be enjoying themselves a great deal and stayed very late. At about three in the morning, when there were very few people left in the club, I saw the King get up and walk over to the disc jockey and then return to his table in the discotheque.

I made my way unobtrusively to the DJ and asked if the King had a problem with the volume of the music.

'No,' he said. 'He asked me if I would play "Dancing Queen" by Abba.'

Abba had written this in 1976 when Carl and Silvia got married as a tribute to her. There was nobody else on the floor of the discotheque. The music started, the King stood up, he bowed to his Queen and took her by the hand. She rose and the two of them danced. It was a truly magic moment.

King Hussein of Jordan (who ascended to the throne when he was only eighteen because his father was deemed mentally ill) used to be a regular at Dollys. He was training at Sandhurst at the time and, with his fellow under-officers, would come to London at the weekends to let off a bit of steam. Hussein had quite an eye for the girls.

On one occasion, years later, when his life was very much under threat, he turned up with ten bodyguards. I said, 'Look, I'm sorry, there's no way you're going to have ten bodyguards. You can have two downstairs and that's it. If you want the others in the street or nearby, that's fine.'

He understood, a very modest and thoughtful man. The last time I saw him was not long before he died. He and Queen Noor came for lunch at the Belvedere, the restaurant I owned in Holland Park. I had met his wife when we went to Stephanie Powers' wedding in Africa – she was there with her sister.

After the royal couple had settled into their table I came out to say hello. The King immediately stood up.

I said, 'Please Your Majesty, sit down!'

That was him, he was such a gentleman. A couple of his sons now come down to the club.

Lots of royals, British and foreign, frequented Tramp. The Crown Prince of Belgium has been coming in recently. Ex-King Constantine of Greece used to be a regular and so was Helen Windsor. She was very quiet and demure but a lovely person, not just in looks. Prince Albert of Monaco would dance the night away with the former Miss World, Mary Stavin.

I always used to get a thrill out of seeing them, especially members of our royal family. I found it a great honour, although

I was always slightly on edge, in case anything untoward might happen. But nothing ever did.

Except once.

It was in the summer of 1972. Prince Rainier and Princess Grace of Monaco were in having dinner with David and Hjourdis Niven. Afterwards they repaired to the discotheque for a brandy or whatever.

I had a strict rule against girls dancing together – as I said, it reminded me of cheap dance halls where women used to dance round their handbags. But I had made an exception in the case of Maria Schneider, Marlon Brando's buttered co-star in *Last Tango in Paris*, who was a leading lesbian.

She always came with Patti D'Arbanville who later had a baby with Don Johnson of *Miami Vice* fame. Don was a good friend of mine, in fact, he, Mickey Rourke, Sly Stallone and I had a riotous boys' night out together in LA – but that's another story. Patti also had a successful career as an actress. Also with them was a very wild Danish girl called Kirsten, who was, at one time, the girlfriend of Jimi Hendrix. To say that these women were dancing erotically would be like stating that the pope is Catholic!

Suddenly Maria spotted the Princess. She ran across and grabbed her by the hand. 'Gracie, come and dance with us!' I managed to get myself over to them and apologised to the Princess, but she couldn't hear me as she was roaring with laughter, a wonderfully throaty, very naughty laugh.

Chapter Sixteen

Any club has to have rules but I always tried to minimise them as much as I could. After all, it was a place for relaxing I was running, not a school or institution.

But antisocial behaviour was out. And I defined that as anything that upset other people. Looking back, with so many rock groups among our early members, it was amazing that I didn't have to ban more of them. There was a tradition in the seventies of groups smashing up their hotel rooms and throwing televisions out of the windows. It was almost expected of them.

But not in Tramp. When I accepted as members people like the members of Led Zeppelin, or Rod Stewart, when he was with the Faces, I used to give them a little lecture. 'Now listen: if you want to be a member of my club, you've got to remember two things. A: you come here to enjoy yourself; B: the first time you misbehave you'll be out of here so fast your feet won't touch the ground. You remember those two, we're going to get on like a house on fire and you'll be more than welcome.'

That was it. I used to make that speech to all those so called hell-raisers, who hardly gave me a solitary problem.

But there is always an exception that proves the need for rules, and it came in the unconventional shape of Keith Howard Moon. The Who drummer had raised hotel-trashing to an art form. Frequently dressed as a court jester, a Nazi officer or a bumblebee, he could dismantle his room in minutes. The Holiday Inn group would call for armed guards at the very mention of the Who.

I was very friendly with Keith. He was a lovely boy but a bit screwed up, like Brian Jones of the Stones. Brian used to sit with me and he would literally, physically cry, he was so churned up and messed up inside. And Keith had elements of this – plus a drink and drug problem the size of the Ritz. But he could control it. Usually.

One evening we were sitting together having a drink. I got up to go to the lavatory, telling him I wouldn't be a moment. When I came back into the restaurant, there was the most enormous crash. I ducked instinctively. I thought I was back in the war.

We had distinctive bell lights on a bar hanging from the ceiling in the restaurant and one had smashed down on to the table beneath. Well, it hadn't just fallen. I quickly learnt that Keith had climbed on the table, grabbed the light, and pulled it from the ceiling.

I asked him, 'What the fuck are you doing?'

He looked at me innocently. 'I'm sorry, Johnny.'

'*You're* sorry? Piss off and don't come back. You are out of here. Out, Keith. How dare you? And, by the way, I want five hundred pounds for damages. Now piss off.'

He left, nearly in tears. About two hours later his chauffeur arrived with an envelope with £500 in it – in 1976 that was a lot of money. Fifty quid would have been a lot. I had just chosen the sum at random.

Keith phoned me the following day. 'Johnny, you're not going to bar me, are you?'

I said, 'Keith, what do you expect? You are barred.'

'Johnny, don't. You can't ruin my life.'

I told him, 'Keith, I've had it. I can't believe what you did to me. How can you show me up like that and show yourself up like that?'

He pleaded, 'No please, please.'

I repeated, 'Keith, you are barred.'

'No please, please.'

He sounded so desperate I relented a little. 'All right, I'm barring you for a month.'

'No, not for a month. I can't stand a month.'

'OK, a week.'

'No, not a week, please.'

So I said, 'Listen, to get you off the phone, forty-eight hours.'

'No. Please, please.'

I stuck to my greatly reduced position. 'Forty-eight hours, that's it. You're barred for forty-eight hours.'

He said, 'What am I going to do?'

'You'll think of something.'

A car arrived within an hour with a beautiful, hand-carved roulette wheel, which sits in my study to this day, and the letter of apology from Keith saying, 'Please forgive me, I'll never do it again.'

Nor did he. Keith was always slightly on the edge and it was just one of those things. He suddenly snapped for no reason. Today, he would probably have got some psychiatric help. But within two years he was found dead – of excess – in his Mayfair apartment. Dead, but not forgotten.

Others parted company from the club for more bizarre reasons. One cult actor in the sixties suddenly decided to take down his trousers in the middle of the dance floor and expose himself to anyone who might be interested – I thought the time had come for me to tap him on the shoulder and say, 'Oi, on your bike.'

The hardest and saddest decision I had to make at Tramp was to ban my friend, George Best. He was a well-intentioned man and the best soccer player I ever saw in my life. It was a great shame that he was Irish because if he'd been English or even Scottish he would have had a chance of playing on the world stage, and that such a talent couldn't appear was not only frustrating for him, it was frustrating for every football-loving person in the world, because they missed out seeing him playing with the greats. David Beckham and today's team don't even hold a candle to George. He could do everything. He was a genius. It was a privilege to call him a friend.

But he had an enemy within himself that is no secret from the world – alcohol.

He would go on binges at various bars in town and then always end up at Tramp. In the winter of 1970, quite soon after the club opened, he came when he had been on a real binge for about two weeks and insisted he was going off to Spain.

I tried to reason with him – he would sometimes listen to me – and then pleaded with him. 'George, don't do it in the middle of the season, please, I'm begging you. Promise me you'll speak to Matt.'

He promised. And he kept his word. The next day he said, 'I'm going back.'

I said, 'You promise me, I'll take you to the stadium.'

But he declined, 'No, no, I swear to you, I'm going back.'

He went back to Manchester on the Wednesday. That Saturday, they were playing Northampton in the FA Cup. He hadn't trained, but he scored six goals.

Next time I saw him I joked: 'You'd better stop training and just keep on drinking.' But he knew I meant the reverse.

I saw George go through all his different girlfriends. When he was with Marjorie Wallace – Miss World – he was accused of stealing her passport and various valuables. The police arrested him in Manchester and took him to London where he was put in the cells and later was let out on bail of £6000. In fact, he was having lunch with me and Marjorie at my other club, Rags, when the robbery took place. The whole thing was just nonsense.

George drank a lot of champagne and he got to the state where he didn't need many drinks to be drunk. One night I was sitting at my table in Tramp having a quiet supper with Michael Caine when George came in drunk. He joined us and drank some more – which he clearly didn't need. So Michael gave him some gentle, avuncular advice on how he should look after himself more carefully.

I saw George's face go white. He stood up and tried to whack Michael. Michael just moved away and all George succeeded in doing was to knock his glasses off. Michael grabbed his arms by the wrists and said, 'Now, George, don't be a silly boy.' Michael can handle himself. George can, too, but George always picks people who are too big, and that's why he gets thumped. He's fearless. Michael told him to sit down. George obeyed him. They shook hands and everything was fine.

The press somehow got hold of it and they made out that George hit Michael and he went flat on his back, plus a whole lot of sensational nonsense, none of it true. But, when George came to write his autobiography, his collaborator must have taken the stuff from the cuttings and put it in as true.

What, in fact, *is* true is that George was too drunk to have any recollection of what happened that night.

The final straw was a girl called Angie Lynn. They had a very volatile relationship, then broke up. She still came to Tramp and she was in one night with Tim Jeffries, who was later engaged to Claudia Schiffer. Tim's a real nice boy whom I had known for years, before he married Koo Stark.

George turned up that night with another girl. I warned him: 'George, I don't want any problems,' and he promised: 'You won't have any problems, Johnny.' He didn't seem to be drinking a lot and they didn't stay for long.

I was sitting talking to Tim and Angie Lynn and, literally two minutes later, George came rushing back into the restaurant and threw Tim Jeffries right off his chair and jumped on top of him. I immediately jumped on George and pulled him off.

I was seething. I said, 'You're out of here, George. This is the final straw. You've done it. You're out of here. I don't want to know any more. You're out!'

I wouldn't let anybody else handle him. I walked him up the stairs and continued: 'How the fuck could you do this to me, George, and how could you do it to yourself, show yourself up like this? If you can't control yourself, I can't have you in here, George. You've upset the whole club and you've upset me particularly. So goodbye.'

He went off and I was absolutely choked. I saw him from time to time outside the club but I wouldn't let him come back.

Two years later I was invited to the launch of his autobiography. In his speech he said, 'I would like to thank Johnny Gold. I really respect this man. He had the balls to throw me out of his own club, although we were friends. I'd just like to apologise and thank him for everything.'

I admitted him back to the club but he wasn't always free to come. I still have a letter he sent me:

HM Prison Ford,
Arundel.
Name: Best.
Number: 76245.

Dear Johnny,

This is the last fucking letter I'm writing from here. I'm glad Victor [Melik – another member who was in for fraud] got some sort of result. I wish I could say the same of Brighton Football Club [he knew I was a life-long supporter]. You probably won't recognise me when I return with the old tan plus 14 pounds that have mysteriously vanished from my frame. I shouldn't use the word frame in here – a few of my new friends get a bit touchy. Give my regards to everyone in the club and keep my seat warm. The beautiful Angela and I are disappearing for a few weeks of sex, sun and sex.

Love George.

Today, he's back – and I hope he will be for a long time to come.

My diary entry for 30 May 1985 reads: 'George Michael [then with Wham!] got so drunk that he was throwing up all over the place. He was really in a state and we had to throw him out and tell him not to come back.'

Some years later, he enquired through somebody whether I'd let him back into the club. I said that of course I would, he's grown up since then. He was young and just didn't know how to handle his fame and everything else that was happening to him.

But he never did come back. Somebody told me he was really nervous of turning up in case I threw him out again.

Being a big boxing fan, I was delighted when John Conteh joined the club. He had an amazing amateur career, winning his first seventeen fights, and his magic and talent continued as a professional. I think he lost only once before he beat Jorge Ahumada to take the WBC world light-heavyweight title.

What a night! The first of October 1974. I went to Wembley to see the fight, before going on to Tramp. Afterwards a party was given for John at the Playboy club. An ex-bunny, Serena Williams, used to do the publicity there (she went out with the football manager, Malcolm Allison, and today she's the general manager of a hotel called Compass Point in the Bahamas, where Jan and I stay). Anyway, Serena phoned and said, 'Johnny, Johnny, Conteh's in a bit of pain. I don't know what's best for him.'

I immediately said, 'The Turkish baths in Jermyn Street. That's the best place.'

She agreed. Half an hour later Guido came over to me and said, 'John Conteh just phoned up and said I'm over at the Jermyn Street Baths, could we bring a bucket of ice and could you bring it personally?'

I said, 'Fine. Guido, do me a favour. Go and get a bottle of Dom Perignon, a very large bucket of ice and four champagne glasses. You're coming with me.'

So Guido and I marched down Jermyn Street, Guido holding the tray with the champagne – this was at about 1.30 in the morning. We walked into the Jermyn Street Baths and there lying on a table was John, swathed in towels, with his manager George Francis. The bruising on his body was just incredible. We opened the bottle of champagne and the four of us sat there and toasted the new light-heavyweight champion of the world. It really was a magic moment.

But John was unwise. He had a contract with the promoter Harry Levine for £10,000 for two more fights, which today would translate into £100,000 – admittedly not a lot of money for a champion of the world.

John later told me, 'My brother says I shouldn't bother with this contract. It's not fair.'

I said, 'You listen to me. If you break this contract, you will never fight in this country again. You'll be very lucky if you fight in any decent venue anywhere in the world because they've got a lot of powerful friends in America. Just realise, there are two fights – you'll fight two bums because that's who they'll put you in with. There won't be anybody that'll be a threat to your title. The ancillary rights, the money that you'll earn from advertising, television and radio will more than make up for the ten grand you're getting paid. Do the two fights, then you can go for a really big payday. But John, don't break the contract.'

Needless to say, he listened to his brother. He broke the contract and ended up fighting in some little town in America, lost his title and had to go and fight in Monaco, and then he had to go and fight somewhere in Yugoslavia – he couldn't fight in America: not in Madison Square Garden, not in Vegas. This destroyed his career. It was an absolute tragedy because he was a talent.

John got involved with Stephanie, the stepdaughter of Jake La Motta (the middleweight champion Robert De Niro played in *Raging Bull*). He had got very drunk on a few occasions in the club and got involved in more and more arguments. Stephanie would gee him up by flirting with other guys and it came to a head when she started flirting with Gareth Hunt (the *Avengers* actor) and Johnny lost his cool. I sadly had to ask him to leave.

He immediately wrote me a very sweet letter in which he apologised to me. I was really sad but I knew I couldn't have him back because I couldn't trust him. He never attempted to come back and, quite amazingly, I have never seen him since. But it really hurt me because I liked him a lot and I watched him ruin his career. It was a tragedy.

Incidentally, to return to Keith Moon, the night Keith died, Ringo came to the club very depressed at the loss of one of his closest friends. He said, 'Let's order a drink for Keith.' The waiter duly brought it and place it by the seat next to mine, where Keith normally sat. Ringo placed a table candle there too. One of my friends, Monty Marks, arrived and went to sit there. Ringo reprimanded him, 'Monty, don't sit there, it's for Keith.' A little later Bill Ofner appeared – never one to follow the gossip of the day. He too went to sit in the same place. When Ringo admonished him, Bill replied, 'Don't worry, I'll move when Keith comes in.'

I think Keith would have enjoyed it.

Chapter Seventeen

The Wimbledon tennis crowd started to come in during the first summer we were open. The trend was started by a successful Seattle entrepreneur, Richard Wiseman. He remains a dear friend – and a trusting one. He came to the club one night straight from a casino and entrusted two envelopes to my safekeeping. He had already had a drink or two and he had a few more and I didn't see him again that evening. But he was back at Tramp the following night.

I asked him if there was anything he wanted to ask me.

'No,' Richard replied, airily. 'Should there be?'

'You might ask me if I still had those two envelopes you gave me with twenty-five thousand pounds in them,' I suggested.

He looked at me in stunned shock. 'Good God, I clean forgot.'

Richard was the agent of Vitas Gerulitis, the American tennis player, and he brought him down to Tramp. Vitas was really a character, very flamboyant with a most magnetic personality and a huge following. If Vitas went somewhere, thirty people would follow him. I don't know what it was, it was just quite remarkable. Girls really liked him – and I did, too. We just hit it off; he was marvellous company. He once told us at dinner that he had been beaten sixteen times in succession by Jimmy Connors at the start of his career, managing to beat Jimmy only on the seventeenth encounter.

'How did you manage that?' somebody asked him.

'*Nobody* beats Vitas Gerulitis seventeen times in succession,' he replied.

He always used to give us great seats for Wimbledon. Oscar would often come with me. Vitas won the men's doubles in 1975 with Sandy Mayer, which led to a night of considerable celebration. But the match everybody remembers was the 1977 semifinal against Bjorn Borg. The game went into the fifth set. Vitas had a break of serve but Bjorn beat him 8–6.

They were close friends and practised together for Wimbledon on the grass at the Cumberland Club. But that semifinal was a nailbiter. Vitas came so close to winning and at the time Borg was invincible. That night, much to my amazement, Vitas arrived at the club – I thought he would be too emotionally drained and exhausted. He came in and I stood up from where I was sitting and we just hugged one another.

I said, 'Oh, man, you were so unlucky, you were fabulous. You should be really proud.'

I started to clap. As soon as I did so, the whole restaurant stood up and started to applaud him. It has never happened before or since. To get to his table Vitas had to walk to the end of the restaurant and, by the time he got there, he was in tears. He reported afterwards in an interview how emotional that made him – he was more emotional that night in Tramp than on the tennis court! He died in 1994 when he had so much life in front of him. An awful lot of people miss him.

I love sports stars. Arthur Ashe was another one – the first black man to win Wimbledon. He was such a gentleman: so unostentatious, so reserved. Arthur would come in very quietly and have something to eat, usually a hamburger. He tended not to dance up a storm or anything like that. I remember him coming to see me and him telling me that he had had a blood transfusion infected with HIV and that he was dying. It was so sad. He was so dignified and brave and a lovely, lovely man.

Yvonne Goolagong – the first Aborigine to win the women's singles – came down after her final. Her image was that of a shy, quiet girl but she loved to dance. She was a very special girl and became quite a regular. She is the third of eight children whose father was a sheep-shearer, but he encouraged her to take up the game when she was only five. When she got married to Roger Cawley, they invited me to the wedding. They subsequently bought a little island off the coast of South Carolina. They were always inviting me and Jan to stay but we never got round to going. I probably should have done. Actually, if I'd accepted all the invitations I've had over the years, I don't think I would ever have been in London. I would have been buzzing all over the world.

My favourite of all the female tennis players was Chrissie Evert. She was absolutely adorable, a fabulous girl. I was very sorry when her marriage to John Lloyd broke up, but she married again and had a family. She went through a very tough time when she was having an affair with Adam Faith. She phoned me one Christmas Eve.

I asked her, 'Where are you?'

She said: 'You won't believe it, but I'm stuck in this one-bedroomed apartment in the King's Road, all by myself.'

Adam had gone back to his wife and family for Christmas. I remember saying to her, 'Oh, Chrissie, talk about the price of love.'

She replied, 'You can say that again, Johnny.'

I told her, 'Listen, you don't have to be alone. You know there's always room on my table. If you want to come down any time, darling, you come down.'

She replied, 'Bless you.'

Martina Navratilova would also come to the club. When we shook hands she had a better grip than most men who shook hands with me.

Now I see the new crop of tennis players. Tim Henman comes

in occasionally. Jana Novotna loves coming to Tramp; we always have a laugh.

When Bjorn Borg first won Wimbledon in 1976 the final was played on a Saturday and they used to have the Grosvenor House Ball afterwards. He came in after the ball with his trainer, his parents and his girlfriend, Mariana, whom he eventually married, and a member called Eric Steiner. Eric, who was also Swedish, had been famous in the fifties and early sixties because he had one of the first casinos in London, called the Pair of Shoes. They sat in the discotheque and Eric, of course, introduced me to them all.

At about two in the morning, Eric called me over and said, 'They're a bit hungry. Could they have some breakfast?'

I told him, 'Of course, we do great breakfasts.'

So I took them into the restaurant and I showed them to the table. They asked me to join them and we all had bacon and eggs and sausages. When it came time to go, Bjorn stood up and held out his hand and we did one of those American handshakes.

I said to him, 'Same time, same place, next year.'

He won Wimbledon the following year, beating Jimmy Connors, and he came down and sat at the same table in the discotheque. Later, at about two in the morning, he said, 'What about breakfast?' And they moved to the same table in the restaurant. At the end of the breakfast I joined them, stood up, we did our same silly handshake and I said the same words. We did that for five consecutive years. In 1980 he won after that incredible fourth-set tie-break with John McEnroe that lasted about twenty minutes.

But that winter, Christmas 1980, the fifth year that he won Wimbledon, he turned up unexpectedly one night at the club. It was the first time I'd ever seen him in the winter. Bjorn greeted me warmly: 'Hi, Johnny, how are you?' But there was something strange about him: he didn't seem his usual reserved self.

He said, 'I'm in the mood to party.'

I said, 'You just might get lucky.'

So he stayed and had a few drinks. I can't remember if he did get lucky or not. But I said to myself: He'll never win Wimbledon again, because this is so out of character compared with the discipline that he always had. Even in winning, he still kept within very strict bounds – he was almost robotic – and here all of a sudden was a side of his character I had never seen. I thought: If he's lost that discipline, then he's lost that will and he'll never win again. And he never did.

Later, John McEnroe used to come down. It was quite funny because his wife, Tatum, hated me when she was a child. She was over here in 1973 promoting the movie *Paper Moon*, in which she appeared with her father, Ryan O'Neal. She played this huckster kid who sold bibles to widows and she won an Oscar for her performance. Ryan phoned me one night and asked me, 'Johnny, do you mind if I bring Tatum to the club?'

I asked him, 'How old is she?'

He said she was ten. I told him, 'Give me a break. I can't have ten-year-olds in the club, even if she *is* a movie star and even if she *is* your daughter.'

So he called out, 'Tatum, Johnny said no' – and I could hear the yell from the other side of the room. Nevertheless, Ryan came to the club frequently. About a week later, I was walking down Bond Street and who should come walking towards me but Ryan and Tatum?

Ryan said, 'Hey Tatum, this is Johnny Gold, you know, the guy who wouldn't let you into Tramp.'

She stuck her tongue out and screwed up her little face in sheer hate towards me. I always reminded her about that in later years.

The marriage of the McEnroes was another that bit the dust. John was very quiet, normal and often genial – unlike his on-court persona. I owe his brother, Pat, a debt because he told me at the start of Wimbledon 1991 to back the German, Michael

Stich. Which I did at the really good odds of 33–1 because people like Becker, Edberg, Lendl, Courier, Agassi and even Pat's brother, John, were playing. I'll never forget watching him play and shouting, 'Come on, Michael.' People were saying: 'Who is this idiot calling for Michael Stich all the time?' But he won the championship.

Ilie Nastase is such a character. He often came down to Tramp and still does. I love him. I used to go and watch him play and I'd be in hysterics. What an absolute talent. He never won Wimbledon but lost one of the classic finals to Stan Smith in 1973. It's so strange: you look at the players today from European countries and none of them have the fun and flair that he had. I find it far more entertaining to watch the oldies like Nastase play than most of our latest lot.

I met Rod Laver on a few occasions. Unlike Nastase, he was very serious when playing but he was very jovial off the court. I never really saw Boris Becker during his formative years at Wimbledon but I did meet him a little later. He'd come down with his wife and they'd dance up a storm – he really enjoyed himself.

Then there are the cricketers – people like Dennis Lilley. He was fantastic. 'Hello, Goldie!' he'd scream in that loud Australian accent when he came into the club. The Waugh brothers joined me for dinner one night – Steve and Mark. They were very relaxed and humorous except when it came to the serious business of Pommie-bashing on the field.

Then there was Lara. Brian's a really lovely guy from Trinidad. I remember he was trying to break the record for the highest consecutive number of centuries – I think it was six centuries on the trot – and he needed one more for the record. He came down to see me the night before and I introduced him to Robert Sangster and some other people who were in the club that night. Eventually he said, 'I'd better go because I'm playing tomorrow.'

He didn't get his sixth century – he was out for 23. Another one ruined by Tramp – not true, actually, because he was only drinking Perrier.

The night before I finished this page, Pelé came down for a drink after being the last person to kick a ball at Wembley before its demolition. He looked in peak condition and spoke much better English now than he did 35 years ago – but I suspect he's a bit slower on the field. Such a self-effacing genius.

Chapter Eighteen

The greatest sportsman of them all was and remains Muhammad Ali. I had followed his career since he won the light-heavyweight gold medal at the Rome Olympics in 1960. After he turned pro, his first fight outside the States, and his last before he removed the world heavyweight title from Sonny Liston, was in London against Henry Cooper in the summer of 1963. Long before James Cameron used the phrase for his *Titanic* Oscar-acceptance speech, Ali announced to the London crowd: 'I am king of the world.'

He had been goaded on by Jack Solomon, who was promoting the event, and thoughtfully supplied him with a crown and royal robe for the weigh-in. Ali said then that Cooper was just a warm-up for the real crown – 'This ain't no jive, Cooper will fall in five.' Which, of course, he did, but not before he gave Ali a real fright. The fight was stopped because Cooper had a terribly cut eye.

In September 1976 Jarvis Astaire invited Jan and me to Ali's world title defence against Ken Norton in New York. Norton was the last man he had lost to. Ali had won seven fights on the trot since winning the 'Rumble in the Jungle' against George Foreman in Kinshasa. He normally won by knockouts, although Joe Bugner had gone fifteen rounds against him in Malaya.

We were thrilled. Not just to see the fight. At the advanced age of 44 it was the first time I'd ever been to New York. The fight was being held at the Yankee Stadium. Jarvis at that time, as well as being Mr Big in British boxing, also happened to be Dustin Hoffman's agent. So, prior to the fight, we went to see a screening of *Marathon Man*, the Laurence Olivier Nazi dentist film with the unwatchable 'Is it safe?' nerve-drilling scene.

I had met Dustin before and we had become quite friendly. We went back afterwards to Dustin's house, one of those brownstones in New York. He took me aside into his study in a high room at the top of the house.

'Johnny, tell me the truth. Was it too violent? Tell me the truth,' he said.

I was used to telling small white lies about movies when their stars came to Tramp but, on this occasion, I thought I would tell him the truth.

'Let's put it this way, if I had a phobia about going to the dentist, this would have really sealed it. But, apart from that, I didn't think it was too violent. I thought the film was great and I thought you were great.'

He seemed relieved.

Later on we went to the fight in a stretch limo: Jan and I, Jarvis and his wife, Commissioner Neil Walsh (who was in charge of all outside events in New York and represented the Black Muslims) and his wife and Sidney Pollock, the movie director. As it happened, at that time, the New York police were on strike. We arrived at Yankee Stadium and drove into the VIP car park. Commissioner Walsh wound down his window and looked out. We were surrounded by black minders, all wearing suits, white-collared shirts and small knotted ties, with arms folded.

Commissioner Walsh said, 'Everybody get out of the car but keep very close together.' Not only were there all sorts of people trying to gatecrash into the arena, but the police themselves were picketing it, thousands of off-duty policemen, black and white, because Mayor Abe Beame had delayed their annual pay rise, owing to a New York budget crisis.

I always had this feeling that something terrible was going to happen to me in New York! Jan knew about this. She was terrified and wouldn't let me out of her sight in the city. Now she was holding on to me, I was holding on to her and the minders were all around us to get us through the mob. It was like the Red Sea opening up. Eventually we got into the arena and up to the commissioner's box in the Yankee Stadium, a luxurious place with a television and everything.

Neil said, 'Look, it's a bit rough out there. Those of you who want to watch it from up here, you're more than welcome.'

Boldly I announced, 'Listen, I have not travelled three thousand miles to come and watch this on television. I want to be sitting ringside because I've never seen a heavyweight championship of the world and to see it in New York is like a dream come true.'

They said, 'Fine. Brother Harry, you look after Mr and Mrs Gold.'

So we followed Harry down to the ringside seats through what seemed like a mass of other fights, with people punching each other. It was an unbelievable scene. Finally we got to our seats in the third row, where we found ourselves sitting next to Sam Spiegel, the producer of *Lawrence of Arabia* and other great David Lean films, whom I knew from Dollys.

He said, 'Johnny, what are you doing here?'

'Same as you, Sam,' I replied.

The fight itself was fantastic. There was no question in my mind that Ken Norton won it. In fact he broke Ali's jaw that night.

I didn't tell Jan but I thought to myself: Shit, if they give this fight to Ken Norton, we're never going to get out of here alive. There will be such a riot.

But they awarded the fight to Ali. I breathed a sigh of relief. Jarvis had told me to remain by the ringside after the fight. So we stood, looking at all the mayhem that was going on. Suddenly Jan pulled me to one side because this whole crowd of black youths – probably the ones who crashed the fight – were charging, hurling chairs as they went, towards the ring, chanting, 'Ali, Ali.'

We took cover under the ring – it was a raised platform – and when we emerged the place had nearly emptied. Certainly the only white faces were mine and Jan's and she's Portuguese Indian, so that left me.

It was truly eerie. We tried to find our way out of the stadium. But two black dudes, one in a white hat and white suit, were making their way towards us.

The guy in the white hat stopped. 'Johnny Gold?' he enquired. It was Butch Wilkins, a big fight promoter from Chicago, who had been to Tramp.

I was so relieved. 'Butch, I've got to get out of here,' I told him.

But Butch was unconcerned. 'Johnny, this is Kevin from WCR radio, Chicago. This is Johnny Gold, he owns the greatest club in the world.'

The guy said to me, 'Would you mind saying something to my audience?'

So, before I knew it, I was giving a radio interview about the fight and Jan was trying to pull me away, saying: 'Are you crazy? We've got to get out of here.'

'How do we get out?' I asked Butch.

He replied, 'Oh, I don't know, Johnny, I've got no idea.' And he just left.

I thought: Well screw you. Next time you want a table, mate, you've got another thing coming.

We made it outside in the dark, feeling abandoned and miserable. Finally we saw a bunch of cops and I asked him where the VIP section was.

He said, 'You'd better be careful round here – ain't no place – '

But his warning was interrupted. A limo came by and stopped, and the door opened. There was Jarvis, ashen.

'Are you crazy?' he demanded, as he pulled us into the car. 'Anything could have happened to you in there.'

That was my first night in New York!

Some years later, who came to Tramp but Muhammad Ali himself? I had never met the man and I was thrilled. His people phoned up and said he wanted to bring a party of twelve people. I told them it was no problem, he could bring the whole Islam nation if he wanted.

I was sitting at my table in the restaurant in Tramp when he came in with his wife Veronica, a very pretty girl. He was holding her mink coat as if someone was going to mug him. I could see he was very uptight. But I also noticed that in the party was an ex-fighter called Jimmy Ellis, who was WBA heavyweight champion of the world for a short time while Muhammad Ali was banned. An older man, now he was his sparring partner.

I stood up and shouted, 'Jimmy Ellis!'

The Alis had gone past me by now, walking towards the end table in the restaurant. But Jimmy Ellis could not believe that someone had recognised him. Ali's head nearly came off his shoulders as he whipped round to see who was shouting 'Jimmy Ellis!'

I went up to him and said, 'Jimmy Ellis, you had the best left jab of any heavyweight I ever saw, like a piston. It was just incredible. I'm Johnny Gold.'

He smiled broadly. 'Oh, you're the owner here. Have you met the champ?'

'No, I haven't.'

'Come on, you've got to meet him. Champ, this is Johnny.'

Ali gave me one of those looks.

I said, 'You know, I have to tell you, I admire you so much.'

He looked at me as if to say: Oh shit, some white boy's going to give me bullshit here.

I went on, 'And the reason I admire you so much – how do you do it? How do you get on an aeroplane?'

Ali loosened up a little. 'You don't like flying?'

'Like flying? I'm just terrified. I know you are, too. But you do it.'

He pulled me down to sit beside him: 'Sit down, Johnny.'

Now, I fly anywhere. I don't care if there's one engine, half an engine, it doesn't bother me at all. But Oscar, God rest his soul, was terrified, and I knew all the symptoms. And I'd read that Ali was terrified.

So I sat with him and, lying out of my head, confessed: 'I get in the plane and the seat is soaking wet from my back.'

He nodded: 'Me too.'

I said, 'I drink, I drink, I'm still sober.'

'Yeah, man, I can't stand the thought of being up there.'

From that moment on, he was mine. 'Why are you carrying that mink coat? Let me get a waiter to take it to the cloakroom.'

He handed it over and seemed infinitely more relaxed.

Afterwards his wife, Veronica, came over and said, 'Johnny, I don't know what you've done. We don't go to white clubs very often – we go to black clubs. But he has not stopped dancing with me all night. What did you do?'

I said, 'Nothing, he likes it here. He's a man of great taste!'

Chapter Nineteen

Jackie Collins wanted to move back to Los Angeles, where she knew there was much fertile material for her novels. And I think Oscar was hankering for his native land a little. So in 1985 they set off for California. As I mentioned, Oscar didn't like flying, so they took the *QE II* to New York, then bundled three kids and a dog into a station wagon and set off across country.

Many of our members were Americans based in London, or visiting from America, and they were always suggesting we open a Tramp in LA.

So we did.

We found some central premises in the basement of the Beverly Center, the landmark shopping mall for Beverly Hills and beyond, which dominates the intersection of La Cienega and Beverly Boulevard.

Oscar had a theatre producer's conceptual mind and, just as he had in Jermyn Street, designed a beautiful club. But this time he was starting from scratch, which made it more modern and striking.

I came over to round up the founder members: with Jackie's help we had few problems getting a strong list – it read a bit like the Academy Award nominations.

As we were getting ready for the opening, the press started

phoning up. Dozens of magazines were desperate to do features on us, but I declined them all.

I said, 'Look, I've got nothing to say about the club, it's a private membership club. There's going to be a restaurant and dancing and that's all I'm going to tell you. There's no opening party. I'm sorry, that's all it is.'

But *Newsweek* persisted. They phoned me and said, 'Mr Gold, we'd like to come to your opening.'

I told them, 'I'm afraid you can't.'

'What do mean we can't? This is *Newsweek?*'

I didn't budge. 'Nobody's coming. It's not a party. Members will come and that's that.'

The man on the phone, their LA correspondent, I think, sounded exasperated. 'Well, can you tell me something about the club?'

'No.'

He exploded. 'Don't you understand who we are? We could open and close this joint, you know.'

I had been running Tramp for seventeen years in London and I just didn't need this.

'You can do what you like,' I told him. 'It's your prerogative.'

He slammed the phone down with the words, 'You goddam Limeys are crazy.'

Maybe we were. But two nights before we opened Oscar and I were watching television and on *Entertainment Tonight*, the main American show-business series, the anchor announced, 'This week, London's most famous and exclusive club Tramp is opening in West Hollywood. People are paying three thousand dollars a year for membership. Sammy Davis has joined, so has Frank Sinatra and Jack Nicholson . . .'

He went on to reel off dozens of familiar names.

Oscar and I looked at each other in absolute astonishment; we hadn't said anything to anybody about the membership.

We opened on 11 December 1984. The pavement outside the

entrance was packed with TV crews and photographers and reporters. You would have thought there was some gala premier of a multimillion-dollar movie. It was quite unbelievable. Oscar and I were truly in a state of shock.

That night remains a blur of faces – not all of them famous – but there was a huge turnout and it proved a tremendous evening. Sean and Micheline Connery were there. Joan Collins came with Peter Holm. There was Shelley Duval, George Segal, Tony Danza, Leslie-Anne Down, Jackie Collins of course, Linda Evans, John James, John Forsythe, Diahann Carol and Frank Sinatra.

What I recall most vividly was that we had hired the most terrible cook. He was a thickset man from Texas and I think he thought he was cooking on a ranch for the cow hands. The food was crap and nearly inedible. As with a Broadway flop, his first night was also his last.

Business then settled down for a bit. A few weeks after we opened, I was having lunch with Michael Caine, who wondered where he should go for a quiet dinner to discuss a movie project with Alan Alda. I suggested Tramp, telling him that Monday was traditionally a pretty dead night.

Michael was an investor in the club so he would be doing himself some good. There was only one other table occupied when I greeted the two men, who were accompanied by Sally Field. 'See, I told you it was going to be quiet.'

A quarter of an hour later Sammy Davis walked in with a group of people. They had no sooner sat down at their table than Robert Culp, who used to be in *I Spy* with Bill Cosby, came in with some people. Robert always claims that I prevented him from committing suicide, so he was effusively friendly. All I had done was to give him a little piece of advice. When he arrived in London his wife had just left him and he was not unnaturally very low. He would sit with me in Tramp night after night and we laughed a bit and he found his world had not come to an end. What I advised him to do was to write down his feelings, in letters to friends or even himself. Very often your problem will end up on paper and not linger inside you. It's not infallible, but with him it worked.

Liza Minnelli turned up with half a dozen friends, and then Dean Martin with his wife, Jeannie, and a whole group of people. After them, Sly Stallone with four friends.

At this stage Michael called me over to his table and demanded, 'Are you trying to take the piss out of me? I wanted a quiet evening, not jumping up and down all the fucking time saying hello to half of Hollywood.'

I crossed my heart. 'Michael, I swear to you, I didn't know. It's the first time it's happened on a Monday night.'

Every single table was taken and every single table had a major star at it. Michael really believed I had arranged it to set him up.

It wasn't all smooth sailing: there was a lot of animosity towards us from somewhere out there. I don't know whether it was from other club owners or exactly what it was, but people were definitely trying to make life difficult for us.

On the tables we used to have red glass candle holders with lighted candles inside. A fire officer arrived, not long after we had opened, and told the manager they were illegal, a fire hazard, and he wanted them removed.

The manager reported this to me later that night and I told him to forget it. About six weeks later the fire officer came back. He was furious. 'I thought I told you to get rid of those lights on the table. I'm coming back in an hour to see if they're off the tables. If they're not, I'm going to arrest you.'

The manager, a polite Southerner, again relayed the news to me. I replied, 'Good, let him arrest you.'

He was more than a little alarmed but I assured him, 'Don't worry about it. It'll be all right.'

An hour or so later, the fire officer came back with another officer with a camera, who started taking photos of the candles.

So far I hadn't spoken to the fire officer but now I walked over – the manager was as white as a ski slope – and I said, 'Can I help you? I'm the owner.'

He was more than a little annoyed. 'I've told your manager these are illegal and I'm not having them here any more.'

I said, 'I see.'

'I've told him I was going to arrest him.'

'Fine. Arrest him.'

'What?'

This was not what he was expecting to hear.

'If you're going to arrest him, arrest him,' I went on, 'but just before you do, your man taking pictures here with the camera, does that show the date and time?'

He said, 'Yeah.'

'Good.'

He was incredulous. 'What do you mean "good"?'

I told him, 'I've got someone within a mile's radius of here, taking photos of candles just like these in restaurants and clubs which have been running in this town for many years and nobody's ever told them it's a fire hazard. Isn't that a coincidence? Now arrest him. Because I want to see when we go to court how it's going to look with your photos and my photos. Now please arrest him, charge him and I'll see you in court.'

He became more aggressive. 'You trying to insinuate anything?'

I shook my head. 'I'm not insinuating anything, but you'd better go back to whoever sent you and tell them.'

Those candles stayed there for the whole time that we had Tramp and nobody ever said another word about it. But they were bastards. They would try so many things to give us a hard time.

I was never quite sure who was behind this sustained inspecting. I knew it wasn't the Mafia. When we were getting Tramp ready, I got a phone call in the club from a guy who, I thought, was an agent or producer in Hollywood whom I'd met.

'Hi, Johnny, I just wanted to welcome you to town and wish you every luck with the club, hope it does well. I just want you to know, Johnny – I don't want anything from you – but just to let you know if you ever have a problem, I'm a phone call away.'

I said, 'Thank you very much.'

I told Michael Caine and Oscar about it the following day. 'I got this funny phone call from Carlo Simonelli.'

They replied simultaneously, 'Whatever he says, say yes to.'

I retorted, 'You are a couple of arseholes, I never knew he was connected.'

Some days later I was invited to a party on the beach at Malibu by the head of one of the studios. *Le tout* Hollywood was there. There were so many gorgeous girls. It reminded me of a David Niven story he told me in Tramp, London. He hadn't been out to Malibu for years and he went to a party there. A stunning girl came up and said, 'Hi, I've always loved you, David, would you like to have a blow?'

He thought: Good Lord, I've just arrived and I'm going to get a blow job. He let her take him outside where she offered him a line of coke – not quite what he had in mind.

That night I was introduced to this huge guy called Vinny. I tried to make conversation but words were not his forte. After I had escaped I asked my host, 'Who was that chap?'

Blandly he informed me, 'Oh, Vinny, he's a Mafia hit man.' All the stars knew him; he seemed to be friends with everybody.

The following day I had lunch at the Bistro Gardens with Oscar, George Hamilton and David Niven Jr. The main course had just arrived when the manager came over and asked, 'Mr Johnny Gold?'

I identified myself and the manager said, 'Mr Arimondi would like to have a word with you.'

I said, 'Fine, I'll just finish my main course.'

Immediately a boot belonging to George Hamilton whacked into my ankle under the table, nearly fracturing my tibia. George smiled at the manager. 'Mr Gold's coming right away.'

I looked at Oscar and he nodded. 'Go!'

Somewhat bewildered, I got up and the manager took me to the back of the restaurant. Sitting there, as though in a scene from *The Godfather*, was this guy in a white suit, with a white hat, and with him was Vinny, who leapt up and gave me a kiss on both cheeks as if I was his long-lost brother, and then introduced me.

'Johnny, this is Don Arimondi.'

I emitted polite greeting platitudes, although I still hadn't a clue what it was all about.

Arimondi took my hand. 'Mr Gold, I've heard from my confederates that you are truly a gentleman and you have been most generous to my friends when they have visited London and that you've always been a perfect gentleman and I just wanted you to know that I would like to officially welcome you here to Los Angeles and to hope that you will be really happy and have great success. We want nothing from you, nothing, please remember this – except your friendship. But, should you have any problems of any nature, we are only a phone call away.'

Trying to remain cool but with my heart thumping, I replied, 'Thank you very much. It was a pleasure meeting you.'

That was it. I never saw that man again – if you made me swear on a stack of bibles who he was, I couldn't tell you.

There was, however, a sort of sequel to that experience. Jan and I were in New York and Mick and Annie Jones invited us to go for dinner to this restaurant on the west side. Mick is the lead singer of Foreigner and Annie was previously married to Gerald Ronson's brother, Lawrence. Now she's the queen of New York society.

Mick enthused about the restaurant: not only was the food out of this world but the place was the haunt of some great characters, not least Frank Sinatra when he was in New York.

Mick was warmly greeted by the manager, Danieli, and duly introduced us: 'This is Jan Gold, Johnny's wife.'

Danieli politely took her hand and then threw his arms around my neck. 'Jesus, Johnny Gold, I can't believe it.'

I had absolutely no idea who he was. But there he was hugging me and kissing me as if I was a long-lost friend. He shouted across the restaurant, 'Marty, you'll never guess what: fucking Johnny Gold is in our joint.'

I was beginning to think – like Michael Caine on Monday night at Tramp – that this was a setup by Mick. Then 'Marty' came running over and threw his arms around my neck. I had no idea who he was, either.

After tactful bluffing and questioning it turned out that the two of them spent a fortnight in London. They were great friends of Dwight Hemion and Garry Smith, two American TV producers whom Lew Grade had brought over to London to mastermind big musical spectaculars.

By now Mick and Annie and Jan had gone to sit at the table and I was still having my hand wrung and being told, 'Do you remember the night...?' which, of course, I didn't but it would not have been politic to say so.

I excused myself, saying I had better join Mick and the ladies.

'No, you're not sitting there,' Danieli insisted. 'You're coming over here.'

He instructed a waiter: 'Move them to table fourteen.'

We went to the table – it was almost on a dais in the corner – and a bottle of Dom Perignon was brought over, courtesy of the house.

Mick looked at me and whispered, 'Johnny, is there something about you I don't know?'

'Like what?'

He said, 'I've been coming to this restaurant for years – this table is only reserved for Mafia dons or Sinatra. No one but no one else sits at this table.'

I gave him a knowing smile. Well, it's good for the image, isn't it?

Chapter Twenty

My main concern was to run Tramp in London, but one week a month on average I commuted to Los Angeles to front up things there. Oscar had been brilliant at shaping the club and filling it with his and Jackie's friends, but it wasn't his style to greet people every night. I suppose by nature he was more of a guest than a host.

I used to try to make my trips coincide with various invitations in LA, the most coveted of which was Swifty Lazar's Oscar dinner. You never called him 'Swifty' to his face – Irving was his real name but he was, by legend, the fastest and the best agent in town to make a deal with the studios for your book.

His Oscar dinner was equally legendary. He took over a whole restaurant – in later years Wolfgang Puck's Spago – and unless you were inconvenienced with an Oscar nomination and had to go to the Dorothy Chandler Pavilion, you went to Swifty's. The invitations were like gold dust. Jackie Collins said if stars didn't get one they would turn off the lights, draw their curtains and pretend they were out of town. The only way the uninvited could get in was to wave a newly won Oscar at the guards on the door after the ceremony.

Swifty – like a whole host of stars and producers and directors – used to make two 'working trips' to London each year. The first was in May on their way to the Cannes Film Festival. The second, in July, was to see the tennis at Wimbledon. They all had friends who were members of Tramp and that was how I met Swifty. I was intrigued to see this little man, like a gnome, with a totally bald head and big, black, horn-rimmed glasses. We got on very well – he was such a character; there was no one quite like him.

If Jan was unable to accompany me – she was often holding the fort at Tramp London – Swifty always said, 'Hey, Johnny, I've put you with some good people.' I sat one year with Walter Matthau and Jack Lemmon.

On another Oscar evening I was walking past a table and Kathleen Turner jumped up and demanded, 'What are you doing here, Johnny?' I had seen her only the previous week in Tramp London with Michael Douglas.

I explained I was trying to spend a week a month in Tramp LA.

She insisted, 'You must have a drink with my friends Meryl Streep and Jessica Lange.' Which I did. When I left them, I walked straight into a wall. I am always stunned to meet stars and there were some huge ones there that night: Audrey Hepburn was there – she looked stunning – Elizabeth Taylor, Walter Matthau, James Stewart, George Burns, Suzanne Plechet, Tom Selleck, Michael and Shakira Caine, John Huston, Cher, Steve Martin, Alan Carr, Johnny Carson, Joan Rivers, Joan and Jackie Collins, George Hamilton, Richard Dreyfuss, Sidney Poitier, Jackie Bissett, Raquel Welch, Carol Burnett, Barbra Streisand, Robin Williams. What a cast – an incredible night.

Today the *Vanity Fair* party at Mortons has tried to take over where Swifty left off.

Swifty was a thoughtful man. He took me to the opening day of the baseball season at the Yankee Stadium, the home of the LA Dodgers, where he shared a box with Gregory Peck. He was in his mid-seventies and he said, 'You've got to have one of these spice dogs' – and these huge chilli hot dogs would arrive. Ghastly. You would think one would kill anybody, but he would eat two.

As we were about to sit down he shouted, 'Steward, steward.'

A harassed-looking man in uniform came speeding over. 'Yes, Mr Lazar?'

Swifty said, 'Look, you want me to sit on this dirty seat?'

There was a minuscule speck of dirt on the seat and, as the man wiped the seat with a cringing 'sorry, Mr Lazar', I thought: I can't see this happening at White Hart Lane.

He told me some wonderful stories. He used to represent Greta Garbo and a huge number of stars, including Humphrey Bogart. On one occasion he persuaded Bogart to do a movie and the actor phoned him up, screaming, 'Irving, you get your ass down here. You've got to get me out of this goddam movie, it's awful.'

So he flew down to Mexico and said, 'Now what's the matter, Bogie?'

'I've got to get out of this fucking film. I'm acting with this blond-haired faggot [William Holden] and a skinny English broad [Audrey Hepburn] and a cockamamie director [Billy Wilder]. Get me out!'

Swifty remained calm. 'Stop yelling and stop screaming, will you. You take your money and do it. It's six weeks' shoot. Stop complaining, Bogie.'

'Fuck you, Irving. It's all right for you sitting there in an air-conditioned Beverly Hills office, but I want out.'

'Just do the movie and don't get yourself excited.'

He left with Bogie still shouting obscenities. So Swifty stopped and turned around. 'You know the trouble with you, Bogie? You're an Aquascutum actor.'

'What do you mean, an Aquascutum actor?'

'Without a raincoat, you're nothing.'

Bogie stormed off. But he completed the movie – *Sabrina* – which later received Oscar nominations for the skinny English broad and the cockamamie director, but not for Bogie.

I sat next to Billy Wilder at Swifty's last Oscar party. He retained a thick Austrian accent although he must have lived in the States for more than fifty years.

He told me, 'You know something, Johnny? This is the toughest town in the world. I have made so much money for the studios [all those wonderful movies he did like *Some Like It Hot, Double Indemnity* and *Witness for the Prosecution*]. But I made a mistake. I made a film that wasn't such a big hit. Suddenly I didn't get quite as many scripts as I was getting and I didn't get quite so many phone calls. Then I made another mistake. I made a second film. This wasn't any good, either. I got less phone calls, fewer invitations. And then finally I made a third film and that was the end. I didn't see a script, I didn't get a phone call. People ignored me and would cross over the street to ignore me. In this town you're only as good as your last record or your last movie. Don't let anybody kid you anything else. They're bastards.'

I used to see Rod Stewart a lot in Los Angeles, too.

He had been a friend for a long time ever since he had been with the Faces and they were regulars at Dollys. Rod cracked the big time in America with number-one hits such as 'Maggie May' and 'Tonight's the Night'.

He and Alana had a magnificent beach house, 'Trancus', near Malibu, where they asked Jan and me to stay. He has a passion for art, especially Art Nouveau, which he collects. They gave a welcoming party for us with Dudley Moore, Mark Gero & Liza, Tina Sinatra, Shakira Caine and Ryan and Tatum O'Neal. I remember Dudley swearing at Alana, so she tipped a chocolate cake in his lap. You don't mess with Alana.

Rod was nearly a professional footballer. Of course his great passion is for Scotland, although he's probably the only cockney supporter of Scotland that there is. Because his dad was Scottish he decided to wave the Scottish flag instead of the English flag. He probably wouldn't admit to it, but his second love is obviously England, when it comes to sport. He loves most sport, except for cricket. Once, back in Britain, I tried to

get him to come to cricket to watch the West Indies on Sunday
– but no way.

One day Alana, Jan and I were driving through Beverly Hills.
Alana is a very glamorous blonde and my wife is a very beautiful
brunette and I was sitting in the back of this Rolls-Royce
Corniche Convertible. As I was thinking what a wonderful life
this was, we pulled up at the traffic lights and from the car on the
opposite side of the lights, someone screamed at me, 'You rich
fucking son of a bitch.'

I shouted back, 'From your mouth to God's ears.'

On the next occasion Alana and Rod over-generously lent us
their house for three weeks. The children were babies and it was
fantastic. I used to get up at seven in the morning and sit on this
huge wooden terrace from which I would watch the birds diving
into the sea to get the fish. He had made sure the very best
bottles of wine from his cellar were on the table every dinner and
used to leave me little notes describing them.

Alana was very pregnant at the time. Rod was recording in the
Bahamas and he said he was coming back because Alana was
meant to pop any day. 'If it happens,' he instructed me, 'you're
going to have to take her to the hospital.'

Now I get lost going round the corner at Marble Arch and Jan
didn't drive, so I lived in dread of anything happening. Rod
arrived back late one night and then, at five o'clock that
morning, which happened to be Labor Day, Alana popped and
Rod rushed her to the hospital without waking Jan or me. We
wondered why the house was empty when we got up and it was
because Kimberly Stewart was born on Labor Day.

He is very close to the children and talks about them with love
and adoration, but I don't know how often he sees them. In the
summer he normally charters a large yacht and takes all the
family and friends with him.

On that trip to LA Jan and I thought we'd try Mexican food,
which we'd never had. Jan loves Indian food and spicy food, so

we went with Oscar and Jackie to this Mexican restaurant. But we didn't have a clue what to order and what we did order looked pretty awful when it came.

I thought: What are we going to do now? And suddenly a voice said, 'Johnny, what are you doing here?'

It was Larry Hagman of *Dallas* fame. He looked at our food and said, 'You can't eat that crap.'

So he asked the waitress to take all the food away and ordered some more. A whole feast of wonderful food arrived. We had the best lunch. Larry left and we thanked him. When we asked for the bill, he had already paid it. It's good to have friends.

Larry used to sit in Tramp with a little hand-held fan to keep the smoke away.

I used to see quite a bit of Peter Langan, Michael Caine's restaurant partner, both in LA and London. Once, I was in Los Angeles having lunch at the Bistro Gardens with Michael and Oscar when Peter Langan spotted me and shouted across the restaurant to me, 'You were wonderful in bed last night.'

I shouted back, 'Oh, was that you?' We got some strange looks from the other diners.

Peter was a one-off. He used to come to Tramp at least four nights a week in his crumpled white suit. He would always sit at one of the end tables nearest the bar and would order a fillet steak and a bottle of Krug champagne. Frequently he would fall asleep on the table. Sometimes we'd have to wake him because we were closing – other times he would wake himself up and stagger out into the night and go to Soho and have Chinese food. This was one of his rituals.

One night he passed out outside the Ritz hotel, and when he woke up there were tyre marks all over the back of his jacket but he had no idea what had happened.

On another occasion he was in a restaurant, where the House of Blues is now in LA. Suddenly two robbers came in with masks on and guns and screamed at everyone to get down on the floor. They were going to blow their brains out and threatened all sorts of mayhem. But the only sound that could be heard was the snoring of Langan, who was now fast asleep on the floor in a drunken stupor.

Some woman brought a dog into Langan's in London. He told her, 'We don't allow dogs in here because they can bite people.'

She primly replied, 'My dog doesn't bite.'

Peter then crawled under the table and bit the dog and, looking up, said, 'Yeah, but I do.'

He was one of these wonderful eccentrics that we love in the UK. The Americans couldn't figure him out at all. There was this restaurant there called Ma Maison, which was particularly fashionable on a Friday lunchtime, when Hollywood would turn out en masse. Langan, who was trying to raise finance to open a restaurant in LA, was suddenly caught short and needed to take a pee. So he took his dick out and peed in one of the flowerpots in the restaurant. He was with all these accountants who were meant to be raising money for him. Sadly, that was the end of Langan's money-raising schemes in Los Angeles.

He's dead now – set fire to himself at home by accident, it was thought. He had a great eye for art, he knew what a restaurant should be, what good food should be and truly understood the theatre of restaurant.

Then there was the night that Frank Sinatra managed to get me as drunk as Peter ever was. The Friars Club in New York roasted Roger Moore at the Waldorf Astoria. I was thrilled that Roger asked me to be on the dais. Jackie Collins was also up there.

So Oscar, Jackie, Jan and I flew to New York. Jan and Oscar sat at arranged tables in the ballroom.

I was put beside Dodi Fayed, directly behind Roger. On Roger's right was Sinatra and on the left Dean Martin. Next to Dean was Angie Dickinson and next to Angie was Cary Grant. It was a unique night – it was funny, it made me cry. I was very proud to see Roger being lampooned by American show-business royalty.

The whole room was absolutely packed – they sold the tables for more than $1,000 a head for a deserving charity. Sitting with Jan and Oscar was Ronald Perlman, who was the head of Revlon, and Jan was wearing this wonderful white suit.

When it came time to start the whole thing, I noticed a waiter stepping on to the dais with a bottle of bourbon for Sinatra and one of vodka for Dean Martin.

I was sitting there nursing a Scotch and I said to Dodi, 'What's going on with all this booze?'

He whispered, 'That's because we can't get waiters up here once the show starts.'

I said, 'Holy shit! We've got to go through this whole thing without a drink?'

He nodded, but the show had been going for about five minutes when Sinatra turned round and asked, 'Anybody want a shot of bourbon?'

I held out my glass and he filled it to the brim. And continued to refill it during the next two hours. By the time the show ended, I couldn't stand up.

I said, 'Dodi, you're going to have to get me off this stage' – which he managed to do.

I got to Jan just as Ron Perlman, in all the excitement and greetings after the event, managed to knock a bottle of red wine over her beautiful white suit.

He was trying to clear it up with his napkin but only making things worse, and he absolutely soaked her.

'You dickhead,' she shouted at him.

Only my Pash would call the head of Revlon a dickhead.

Oscar said, 'Jan, you can't call the head of Revlon a dickhead.'

I had known Roger since before he became the Saint in the sixties. He had been a lieutenant in the army, so I frequently felt obliged to salute him. The wonderful thing about him is that, although he was a classically trained actor at the Royal Academy of Dramatic Arts, he always made light of his gifts. But he managed to convert his sense of humour with great timing into James Bond, an underrated part of the success of those films.

Our family always used to try to get down for a few days' holiday with Roger and Luisa in the South of France each summer. They had a home near St Paul de Vence and we would stay in the nearby splendour of the Colombe d'Or.

One summer when our sons, Christian and Nicky, were both about twelve, the four of us went out in his boat. We moored it in one of the bays so that the boys could go and rent jet skis.

Roger and I were lying on the boat drinking a couple of beers and I could see a pedalo coming towards us – with four topless girls on board.

I mentioned this to Roger and suggested, 'Why don't we invite them up for a beer?'

'Are you crazy?' he replied.

To our amazement the girls came up to the boat and one of them asked, '*Excusez-moi, quelle heure est il?*'

I told her what time it was and whispered to Roger, 'Are you sure?'

He was trying to keep low down below the gunwale, 'Yes, I'm sure.'

The girls were clearly waiting to be asked up on the boat but, in my best French, I bid them *au revoir*.

I told him, 'You're such a shmuck, Rog. We could have had a giggle with them.' (In case you don't know the meaning of shmuck, it's someone who gets out of the shower to have a pee.)

A week later I was back in London after the holiday. Roger called up and said, 'You arsehole, you wanted those girls to come up on the boat. I warned you.'

There was a picture in *Paris Match* of Roger and me drinking beer with our potbellies hanging out. The four girls had obviously been set up to get on board the boat to make a great scandal of the whole thing.

A lesson learnt – the price of fame, something Roger has put to endless good use as an ambassador for UNICEF. I hope he gets his just reward – a knighthood. He works so hard for UNICEF and does much for the impoverished children of the world.

Chapter Twenty-One

In the early years Jan would come to the club with me nearly every night. God bless her, I don't know how she did it. My children, even as babies, never ever woke me up. Before 11 a.m. Nicky and Claire seemed to know there was to be no yelling and screaming. Don't wake Daddy! And they never did. Mind you, I am a pretty heavy sleeper, having being brought up in the war with bombs and commotion going on all around me. I used to wait until after the bar closed, around 3 a.m., and sometimes after 3.30 a.m., when all the alcohol would be taken off the tables, before I set off for home. A lot would depend on who was in the club. If I thought there was someone who might create a problem in any way I might stay until four.

Even in the club's second decade, one had to be eternally vigilant to keep the right mix of members. I've watched other clubs slip right off the map. One of the vital ingredients was my list of girls who became members in their own right and very much part of London's social scene at that time. Today they call them 'It' girls, borrowing an expression that was first used about the Hollywood star, Clara Bow, in the Roaring Twenties.

The eighties brought a new mix of members, as well as the old stagers. Some of the more memorable gatherings made it into my diary. Michael Caine flew in from Dublin to have dinner with me after filming *Educating Rita* with Julie Walters, a film for which he got an Oscar nomination and should have won.

On 16 May 1983 I changed the staff uniform at Tramp. They used to wear white polo-neck sweaters and the head waiters and manager wore a blazer with a white polo-neck sweater. I took them out of the polo-necks and put them into shirts and ties and waistcoats, which was a huge move. They looked very stylish and I think it proved lucky as well. Liza Minnelli was in concert that night at the Apollo, Victoria. Later, she and Mark, Rod Stewart, Elton John, John Schlesinger, Michael Winner, Terry O'Neill, Michael York and many more came back. They said they liked the new look but were amazed that I would change anything.

Mel Brooks virtually lived in Dollys and, later, Tramp when he was in London. He always loved an audience to perform to and found a ready one here. He used to tell stories about it on television chat shows. In *An Evening With Mel Brooks* on LWT he picked on me and told the audience about the night he threw up over an Indian woman. It was a splendid fabrication. He would frequently crawl around the club on all fours barking like a dog. I never found out why but the members eventually got used to it.

Other stories related to his (professed) drunkenness: 'I woke up in a daze on the floor of the club. Staring down at me were two angel-eyes that occupied the craggy, lived-in face of John Gold,' he once wrote. 'John picked up my drunken Jewish body, threw me into his brand new silver Jensen and drove me back to my hotel. He took off my Keds sneakers and tucked me into bed – as he has done countless times since. But don't get me wrong: John Gold isn't gay; he's just happy.'

All of it lies, of course – except the not-being-gay bit. I'm delighted that Mel has had such a big hit with *The Producers* on Broadway. He is truly one of the funniest and most talented men I know.

Margaret Trudeau had a spell of coming to Tramp after she

separated from the Canadian Prime Minister, Pierre. She was a wild woman and I adored her. She reinvented herself with her own chat show and an exercise class in Ottawa. I made an appearance in a documentary they did about her on Canadian television. She now spends a lot of time in Africa, very deeply involved in finding fresh water for villages that don't have any.

John Denver was in town for two weeks of concerts in the early eighties. He would come down afterwards, obviously frothing for a girl, but less successful than Julio Iglesias, who would get a kiss from every girl in sight.

There were memorable nights off, too. In November 1982 Pash and I went to Paris, where Dodi Fayed arranged for us to stay at the Ritz hotel. We were all there to attend a gala at the Moulin Rouge for Save the Children. Liza Minnelli arranged our table right on the stage. There was a party afterwards at Regines where, being off duty, we got pretty drunk. But it was the night when Dodi announced to me that he'd given up drink.

I said, 'Dodi, I don't trust people who don't drink or don't smoke or don't gamble. They have to do something.'

He looked at me and said, 'I'll have a vodka.'

Back at Tramp, Joan Collins called me in the early hours of Sunday morning from Los Angeles asking me to read her what the newspapers had to say about her boyfriend, Peter Holm. It wasn't good. There were a lot of stories that he was a jewel thief and he was no good and his ex-girlfriends all said Joan was welcome to him.

Joan giggled down the phone at all these stories. When I came to say goodbye to her, I said, 'Give Jackie my love and all the other people in LA.'

She said, 'What about Peter?'

'Ask him if he's got any cheap jewellery.'

'Fuck you!' she retorted, and the phone went dead.

There was an article in the papers, at the time, about two schoolgirls who went missing from the North of England. They were about eleven years old and it said that the last thing they said to their friends was that they were going to London because they wanted to go to Tramp. Luckily the police found them, safe and sound.

Annie Lennox of the Eurythmics once told me, 'I can't believe it, I'm here in Tramp.' I often forget that a lot of these artists grew up reading about Tramp when they were at school and suddenly they find themselves *in* Tramp. I get it a lot from just ordinary customers: 'I remember when I was at boarding school, we used to sneak our lights on and read about what was going on at Tramp.'

Well, they didn't read about everything that was going on. Take, for instance, Robert Wagner (known by all his friends as RJ), who was sitting talking to the producer John Daly, on the little couch as you come down the main stairs. What started as a strong discussion, needless to say about money, took on a different dimension when suddenly John Daly threw a punch at RJ, who tumbled back on the couch.

John shot up the stairs as if there was a rocket up his bum. RJ hurtled after him with me in slow pursuit. By the time I got outside into Jermyn Street, John had run off down the road at full pelt, with RJ still running after him.

John got into his car and RJ attempted to shatter the window with his elbow as the producer backed off. How he never broke his elbow I don't know, because he really was smashing, but the lights changed and off Daly went.

RJ returned rubbing his arm. 'All I wanted to do was to have just one punch. I hate somebody getting just one punch off me.'

At the other end of the scale, one of the amusing raconteurs in Tramp, and also a good friend, is Jeremy Lloyd, the writer of *'Allo 'Allo, Are You Being Served?* and *Rowan and Martin's Laugh-In*. Jeremy can have me in hysterics more than anybody else. He wasn't always as successful a writer and at one stage took a job doing scripts for the elderly Jimmy Clitheroe. He rang him up in Lancashire to see what he thought of the first one and Clitheroe's mother replied, 'He can't come to the phone, he's finishing his fish.'

Jeremy didn't hear anything for a couple of days, then rang again and asked, semi-sarcastically, 'How big a piece of fish is it?'

'Well, he certainly can't come to the phone now,' his mother replied, 'because he's dead.'

On another occasion he met a woman in a bar in Los Angeles who showed him some photographs of extraterrestrials and asked him if he would like to meet them. Jeremy agreed and went with her and a couple of Oriental gentlemen to the top of Look-Out Mountain, where they donned pointy gold helmets and waited for their friends from Venus to arrive. And waited and waited.

A confirmed bachelor in the true sense of the term, Jeremy had a way with women. When he was doing *Rowan and Martin* he went to stay with Julie Newmar, who had been Catwoman in *Batman*, and she provided him with no end of exotic treats.

He spent an enjoyable three-week skiing holiday with Charlotte Rampling, where he was banned – I never found out why – from the slopes of Zermatt; and he was married for slightly longer to Joanna Lumley, whom he met in *The Breaking of Bumbo*, Andrew Sinclair's film about the Guards, memorable for the fact that it was never released.

I introduced Jeremy to an American girl called Collette Northrop in the club one day. I found her endearing because she was a complete and total lunatic. She was having a bit of a ding-dong with Jack Nicholson for a little while as she was working for him in his movie *The Three Jakes*, the sequel to Roman Polanski's *Chinatown*.

Jeremy rather liked her and one Christmas he was feeling a bit cheesed off and lonely, so he suddenly phoned her out of the blue and asked her if she'd like to go away for a couple of weeks with him.

She agreed. He flew to Washington and took her off to South

America, where he fell madly in love with her and married her. It turned out that she was now a lion tamer – the first inkling Jeremy got of this was when she arrived at their wedding with a wild panther. When they went on honeymoon she brought a leopard in a trailer behind the car.

The marriage lasted a little longer than the one to Joanna – but not much.

He dedicated his autobiography – *Listen Very Carefully, I Shall Say This Only Once* – to me. 'For my dear friend, Johnny Gold, for a thousand chats.' I really miss those chats; they were great times.

When Robert De Niro came into the club he usually went and sat anonymously in the discotheque at my table. One evening Guido mentioned he was in so I went to say hi to him.

'I'm having something to eat with Mel Brooks,' I told him. 'Come and join us.'

He protested: 'No, no, it's too bright in there.'

I said, 'Don't be silly, you'll be fine.'

He shook his head. 'No, I'm fine here.'

I went back to join Mel but after less than five minutes I looked up and there was De Niro standing there. I invited him to sit down and introduced them to each other.

Bob said, 'You're right, it's all right in here.'

We all get on like a house on fire. Now of course he's quite happy to come and sit in the restaurant but, up until that day, he thought it was something quite forbidding.

I find him fascinating when he gets talking on cinema or theatre. Being very shy, he would never dream of chatting up a girl he didn't know. One evening, however, after sitting with me for a couple of hours in the disco, he decided to go back to his hotel.

Not long after, Guido came to tell me he was on the phone for me. 'Hey, Johnny, it's Bobby. There was a girl in a red dress at the other end of the discotheque from us. Can you go and ask her if she'd like to come and have a drink with me at the Savoy?'

I said I would go and have a look and returned with the problematical news.

'I'm sorry, Bobby. There are about six girls in red dresses – three blondes and three brunettes. If I make a pick, I'll lay two to one I've got the wrong one.'

Jack Nicholson was at the club virtually every night when he was making *The Shining* in 1977 and again in 1988 when he was back to play the Joker in *Batman*. Jack will often come by himself and sit with me. Sometimes he might come with a couple of friends from LA and sometimes with the English producer, Michael White. But, more often than not, he was on his own.

Jack is unbelievable. He used to leave the club at 3.45 a.m. and go straight to Elstree or Pinewood Studios, have a shower when he got there and go to work. In *The Shining* when his character starts going really mad, Shelley Duval had bloodshot red eyes, she was crying so much all the time for the movie; but Jack would just wander straight on to the set in those days and do his bit.

I always remember him coming and bitching like mad: 'That Kubrick's going to drive me crazy Johnny. I did twenty-seven takes of a scene today. *Twenty-seven.* Do you think it's anything to do with my lines? Nothing. Do you think it's anything to do with the lighting or anything technical like that? Nothing. Do you know what it was? The angle at which I held my whisky glass. Twenty-seven goddam takes. If you see the movie, you won't even care. "Shit, have I got the J & B up there or down there?"'

People in the club didn't used to take a whole lot of notice of him but after he played the devil in *The Witches of Eastwick* in 1986 all that changed. Jack became a sex symbol. I've heard with my own ears women of eighteen or nineteen saying, 'God, I'd like to fuck his brains out' – and they weren't talking about me! It happens all the time; I pretty well have to put a rope round the table when Jack's in.

Jack was great friends with Michael Douglas, who became a friend of mine. When he was over here making some crummy war movie called *Shining Through*, he used to come to the club with his co-star, Melanie Griffiths, and also Goldie Hawn, who was working in London.

Melanie was married to Don Johnson at that time and Goldie was with Kurt Russell. The girls would never tell them they were out with Michael because of his reputation where women were concerned. So they would say, 'We're eating with Johnny' and I would get these transatlantic phone calls.

Don would demand, 'What's going on with you and my wife, Johnny?'

I said, 'Nothing. She's here with Goldie Hawn. We're just having a meal.'

Michael and Melanie were invited to go to a Royal Command performance at the Palladium and they were sitting in the stalls. At the interval somebody came along and asked, 'We wonder if you would like to have a drink with Prince Charles.'

Which they did. And Charles invited them to see the rest of the show from his box. When Shirley Bassey came on and sang, 'There's No Business Like Show Business', Michael leant back in his chair, looked at Melanie and whispered, 'Yes!'

Fame is certainly a passport that opens many doors.

In the late seventies I was friendly with Freddie Laker. He started his own transatlantic airline to take on the big international monopolies. He asked me to be guinea pig, so Jan and I went flying to America and he quizzed us about what we thought of the flight.

It was fine. The only thing I thought was unfair was that the stewardesses had to sleep on the floor in the galley – they had four hours off – and I suggested they put some cots or something in there. I think he did.

Freddie and I became very friendly over the years and,

whenever I was going to America, I would phone up Freddie and make the reservation. Oscar overheard me one day and he went into hysterics when I said, 'I'll have a window seat please, Freddie. And, yes, smoking please.'

Oscar remonstrated, 'I can't believe you've spoken to Freddie Laker, using him like a booking clerk!'

At first he thrived magnificently – less well-off people were able to holiday in Florida for the first time. But then, of course, they ground him down. By early 1982 it looked as if he was going to go bankrupt.

One night he came into Tramp and introduced me to a band of bankers, lawyers and executives. He was emotional: 'Johnny, stand up, give me a hug. These are the people who have saved me from bankruptcy.'

He ordered bangers and plenty of Krug! I sat down and joined them. Everybody was cheering and toasting the fact that Laker Airways was saved.

He said, 'Johnny, I'm going to New York in the morning to do a commercial. I'll be back on Thursday and we'll have dinner.'

'It'll be great to see you, then,' I enthused.

But, on the Wednesday, I was driving along in my car and I heard on the radio that all Laker aeroplanes had been grounded. I thought: What are they talking about? They're mad. I was there when the rescue was done, all signed and sealed.

Freddie later claimed that these self-same men colluded to pull the rug from under him four days later. They had been in on Monday night and on Friday 5 February 1982, Freddie Laker was made bankrupt. I couldn't believe it.

But not only was there collusion: the pound collapsed against the dollar, and the price of oil suddenly shot up. It was like a double whammy for him. He had ordered new aircraft, which was going to cost him more money because he was paying in pounds, and fuel was suddenly going through the roof. So that was what hit him, not bad management or his own fault.

It was then that the big carriers moved in and Freddie sued them for collusion. His lawyers asked me if I would be a witness because I had been present when these people allegedly saved him. I readily agreed. The case took place in Washington but I was never actually called because it collapsed beforehand and they paid Freddie out. Several million dollars. He deserved it.

On 3 November 1983, Ed Bradley of *60 Minutes*, the TV show in America – like our *Panorama* – interviewed me for the programme and it was great to be able to state what an honourable and well-meaning man Freddie was, and tell the story of that night in Tramp.

Chapter Twenty-Two

During the late seventies and early eighties they made a trilogy of successful *Superman* films at Pinewood and Tramp was home from home for the visiting Americans, especially Christopher Reeve, the young soap star who went from daytime TV to international fame.

Christopher was someone we saw become a star, a status that seemed his almost by divine right with his classic looks and stature. At the same time, with his Yale and Juillard background, he was usually more keen on talking politics than show business.

He fell for a warm and graceful English model, Gae Exton, and they had two children, Matthew and Alexandra. Chris and Gae became very much part of the Tramp family and I rounded up some friends and gave a thirtieth-birthday party for him in September of 1982 – Richard Pryor, Bill and Astrid Wyman, Dennis Waterman with Rula Lenska (his new love, after he had recently left his wife), the director Dick Donner and Mel Brooks in a borrowed stetson, glasses and a false moustache. Frank Carson joined in the fun. It was an evening full of much mirth and goodwill.

Thirteen unlucky years later, as the world knows, Chris was thrown from his horse and became a quadriplegic. Gae and the children flew to visit him as soon as the hospital allowed and one of the first things he said to her was, 'How's Johnny?'

'Johnny who?' she asked.

'Johnny Gold. Don't you remember that wonderful surprise birthday party he gave for me in Tramp?'

Gae phoned me from the hospital to tell me this and asked me to send Chris a fax, which, of course I did, saying, 'I'm looking forward to greeting you when next you come walking down the stairs of the club.'

And I wouldn't bet against his doing it – he's got bigger balls than any man I know.

Inevitably, many other tragedies have visited Tramp over three decades (I will write about Dodi and Diana later), but none so close to home as that of Katie Kass, the daughter of Joan Collins, who, after her divorce from Tony Newley, had married Ron Kass.

It's an awful feeling when you are told the police wish to speak to you on an urgent personal matter. I was in Tramp when just that message came. My first thought was that something had happened to one of the children or Jan. I felt sick to my stomach.

But the sergeant at the other end wanted to know where Joan Collins was. I asked why and he said that her daughter, Katie, had been hit by a car and was in a coma. My stomach sank again – I had known little Katie since the day she was born. I asked how serious it was.

'At this stage we can't tell,' came the ominous reply.

It showed great initiative that the police had telephoned me to find Joan. She usually came to Tramp when she was in London. But she had gone to Paris and I didn't know where. I took the relevant police and hospital numbers and promised I would track her down.

I rang all the friends we had in common, but nobody, not even her brother, knew where she was. But then, on a hunch, I rang the home of the folk singer whom her father had managed, Roger

Whittaker. He was in Paris, too, and his wife said he would find her: Joan was rarely inconspicuous.

Not only did Roger find her, but he flew her back to London that night in his private plane. She was at Katie's bedside by dawn.

And there she stayed. The hospital didn't have any facilities for parents and, when Jan and I went to visit, Joan was living virtually in a broom cupboard. In truth, Joan and Ron hardly left Katie's side during that time. They had blessings from rabbis and priests and vicars, praying that she would come round.

The usually glamorous Joan lived in the hospital without a trace of make-up – when we went to the canteen for a cup of tea people would whisper audibly, 'There's Joan Collins', but you hardly care about your public image when your daughter is dangerously injured. Thank God Katie survived and she's turned into a wonderful woman.

As I mentioned, I tried to divide my time between Tramp London and Tramp LA and so did many of our star guests.

They all had different styles. Telly Savalas would be effusively friendly to strangers and make himself very available. As would Jack Nicholson. If a girl I know comes to the table and I introduce him to her, Jack will always stand up and exercise his innate charm.

But you get some of the other ones who don't want to be so sociable. You even get a star like Richard Dreyfuss, who would sit there quietly having dinner and nobody would even know he was in the room even though he played the lead in *Jaws* and had won an Oscar.

The first time Dustin Hoffman happened to come to the club Jan was very pregnant, expecting our son, Nicky. Dustin didn't return to England for a couple of years but when he did he came down to Tramp. Jan was again pregnant, this time with Claire.

Dustin announced, 'This is the longest pregnancy I've ever

seen.' So he advised her: 'You've got to push down like you're going to fart.'

'Thank you, Dustin,' she smiled. 'I had been waiting for your expert advice.'

I remember Dustin shouting at me one memorable day on Malibu Beach. I need to go back a little bit. Every year I would send members a Christmas card with, modestly, a picture of me on it. On the first, naturally, I dressed as a Tramp in Trafalgar Square. From then on Terry O'Neill, dear friend and legendary photographer, delighted in putting me in the most embarrassing positions possible: in tits and tights with a long blonde wig or naked on a rug except for a cigar and tennis socks.

This particular year he had me clothed, wearing a very formal suit and tie, but on top of a sand dune on Malibu Beach in the heat of the day. Mad dogs and Englishmen! Actually, we had a mad dog with us in the shape of Dodi Fayed's Afghan, Hero, who used to mistake me for a lamppost, to his master's immense amusement. Dodi had rented the Malibu home of Sharon Gless (of *Cagney and Lacey* fame) that summer.

After the shoot Terry, Dodi and I took Hero for a stroll along the beach when a voice yelled out of nowhere, 'Johnny Gold!'

I looked up and it was Dustin on the balcony of his house.

'What are you doing here dressed up like a prick?' he demanded.

'My Christmas cards,' I yelled back.

'Well, it's my birthday,' he said. 'Come up and have a drink.'

We duly did and Dustin enthused, 'My wife's just bought me the most brilliant present.'

'What's that?'

'A tennis match with Jimmy Connors. I'm playing Jimmy for my birthday present.'

I said, 'That sounds more like punishment to me.'

'What do you mean? It's going to be great,' Dustin replied enthusiastically. 'But I think I'll let him win.'

I think that, of all the American actors who came to the clubs, the one the girls hit on like crazy was Sylvester Stallone. And, if he liked what he saw, he would invite them to join him. This was before he married Brigitte Neilsen.

'What till you see what I'm bringing tonight, Johnny!' he enthused over the phone.

Indeed, when she walked into the restaurant, the Danish model turned more than a few heads with her Amazonian body.

But the marriage fizzled out after less than three years and, before he settled once more with Jennifer Flavin, Sly was a true, born-again bachelor.

I liked him a lot. He's a sport. I always found him very down to earth, almost taking the mickey out of himself. He was so determined to make *Rocky* and he wouldn't let anybody else touch it, even though he needed money. I just love those stories. These guys who pull themselves up by their teeth and achieve their dream. That's why I like fighters so much. I admire them so much, what they go through to get there. And sportsmen generally – to achieve what they have to achieve – need discipline. Sure, they can have a God-given talent, but so many abuse that talent. The ones that don't, and have gone on to make it to greatness, I really warm to when I see them.

Sly invited me to dinner in Los Angeles in the autumn of 1982. He knew I was as mad about boxing as he was and he thought he had found a great white hope. This was a heavy-weight called Lee Cantrello. Before we ate he came and picked me up to take me to the gym so I could see what I thought of him in training. I asked if he minded if my partner came and he said that of course he didn't. So Oscar and also my young son Nicky went out to watch this Lee Cantrello train.

Unfortunately, he turned out to be a real bum. He was a big, blond guy who just didn't have the talent. He never made it as a fighter. I think he ended up doing some film commercials. That was Sly, though – utterly passionate, really into it.

It would be wrong to give the impression that I was great chums with all the stars who frequented the club. Some were passing acquaintances. The *Star Wars* crowd came down when they were filming at Elstree in north London and Harrison Ford was extremely shy. I remember thinking: This will probably be a one-off movie for him. But that Mark Hamill is going to be a great big star.

Which goes a long way to explaining why I run a club and restaurants and am not a movie producer. Harrison became just about the most bankable leading man for the next 25 years.

But I never really saw Harrison again after *Star Wars*. By sheer coincidence the distributors of his film, *Six Days, Seven Nights* with Anne Heche, decided to hold a post-premiere party in a restaurant I owned, the Belvedere, a couple of years ago.

Harrison was there with his wife, Melissa Mathison (whom I had never met: he married her in 1983, the year after she wrote *ET*), and their children. I didn't want to bother him by reminding him of evenings more than twenty years ago. He must have met thousands of people since then. But he came straight across and said, 'Johnny, how are you?' and introduced the family. I was truly thrilled. It proved what I had always thought of him: what a fabulous guy he was and how down to earth.

That 'do you remember me?' thing happens to celebrities a lot. I've watched it take place so many times. You'd be sitting with a celebrity and somebody will walk in and say, 'Oh, do you remember? I had a drink with you. It was in the South of France in this bar and you came in and you sat next to me, and we had this drink, and you said "nice meeting you" and off you went. It happened fifteen years ago.'

Now the person is always going to remember the night they had with a celebrity, just as I'll always remember the night I got drunk with John Wayne. But it is rarely true for the celebrity involved.

One night in Tramp LA, I was with Elizabeth Taylor and Joan Collins – a nice twosome to sit between! Elizabeth had come with

George Hamilton that night and if I remember correctly Joan was by herself. She'd just phoned up and asked if she could join us and she did – maybe she was with her PR guy, Jeffrey Lane.

A member from London came in, looked over at the three of us, said, 'Only Johnny Gold!' and walked off again.

Elizabeth was greatly amused by this. She was saying how people really think you will remember a minute encounter that took place twenty years ago.

So I pulled one out of the hat. 'I'm going to do exactly that now because do you remember I met you at the Metropole Hotel in Brighton? I think you were twelve at the time, and you were doing that movie about the Grand National – *National Velvet*.'

She thought I was joking. 'You didn't.'

I promised her: 'I did, actually. I grew up in Brighton. We're the same age.'

As we were having this conversation, a guy walked over and said, 'Oh, Miss Taylor, I'm sorry to bother you, but do you remember...?' and we both spat out our drinks. The timing couldn't have been more perfect.

Elizabeth has lived in pain for so many years. She said in today's world they would never have operated on her back – they would have manipulated the slipped discs back into place instead – and that was what had ruined hers. Nowadays, it's all done by manipulation and massage. She told me to feel her back. I put my hand on the small of her back and it was like a lump of metal. She said, 'This is what happens – it suddenly goes into seizure. And then there's this pain.' She's on pain killers virtually all the time.

But she still has these wonderful eyes and that great voice – for me one of the biggest turn-ons is a woman's voice. I love it. I fell in love with Jan's voice first. You can see the most beautiful girl in the world and then she opens her mouth – oh, my God, that's the end of the story as far as I'm concerned. When you hear these wonderful voices like those of Liz Taylor and Claudette Colbert, whom I once had lunch with, you just go weak at the knees.

I've always had a fairly gravelly voice myself and one evening Tom Selleck came into the London club with Al Ruddy, the producer of *The Godfather*.

From then on Al always used to say to me every time he saw me, 'I'm going to put you in one of my goddam movies. You've got a great face and a good voice.'

I made little of it but he came in again with Tom Selleck and told me he was doing a movie in London called *Lassiter* with Tom, Lauren Hutton and Jane Seymour.

He arrived at the club the following night and introduced me to a guy called Roger Young, to whom I chatted affably enough for about half an hour. I excused myself and went off to attend to some business in the discotheque.

As I was passing through the restaurant some time later, Al Ruddy told me to sit down. 'You've got the part.'

'What?' I didn't know what he was talking about.

'In *Lassiter*. This is the director.' He indicated Roger. 'Now you've got to give us twelve free days. Can you do that?'

'Sure,' I immediately agreed before he had a chance to change his mind. 'Just one question: what is it I'm meant to be doing?'

Roger intervened: 'You're playing a casino boss who was once a murderer.'

'Perfect casting, I suppose, for me.' I smiled. 'By the way, I can't act.'

'Don't worry,' Al reassured me. 'Nearly all your scenes are with Tom. He'll help you, you'll be fine.'

They made the movie – but not with me. Needless to say, Equity said the only way I could be in the movie was if I played the part of myself, and, since this spy movie took place during World War One, it would be very difficult to have Johnny Gold opening Tramp in 1915. So, once more, my acting career went out of the window.

Jackie Collins, on the other hand, looked like she was going to make a great deal of money without having to write a word.

One of those porno magazines in America had a blonde on the cover and a headline that ran: 'Jackie Collins, authoress of *Hollywood Wives*, pictured as you've never seen her before!'

When you opened up the centre page, there was this girl, totally naked with her legs so wide open that you could see what she had for breakfast. Underneath it stated it was Jackie Collins.

Jackie's lawyers immediately got on to the publisher, Larry Flynt, to get an injunction. He ignored this and went ahead with distributing the magazine. So they went to court. Jackie was put through a lot of pressure when she had to give evidence.

After she came out of court, she phoned me and said, 'I won. Are you standing or are you sitting?'

'I'm standing.'

She ordered: 'Well, sit down. Guess what I was awarded.'

'I don't know – five million dollars?'

'*Forty* million dollars – the biggest single award for libel.'

We whooped across the Atlantic, preparing for the biggest party Tramp had ever seen.

But Flynt appealed. On the appeal damages were cut down to $10 million. They then appealed again and it got thrown out. Nothing. Jackie was then told to go to the Supreme Court. She went and she lost. So from getting $40 million, it ended up costing her something like $200,000 in legal fees.

American justice baffles me.

At the end of the eighties Oscar was beginning to experience bouts of an unexplained illness. Sadly, it was eventually explained: cancer.

He became progressively more and more ill and was unable to go to the club, although he literally lived just round the corner. I would fly out every four weeks and spend four weeks here and two weeks there – it was killing me – and, while I was there, everything was fine and, as soon as I came back, everything wasn't fine.

In the end Oscar said we had better sell it. So we did, to a former Italian waiter called Giancarlo Parretti. His cheque went through OK but it later transpired that he had an extensive criminal record and had bribed Credit Lyonnais bankers to lend him $2 billion to buy MGM. When he was charged with this, he jumped bail and fled to Italy, where they just arrested him not so long ago. So I think he'll be spending quite some time inside.

The good news was that we got paid. *Newsweek* asked me how I got on with Parretti and I said, 'Listen, I had nothing to do with him. It was all done by lawyers. I never met the man, so I couldn't tell you anything to help you.'

The sad thing is that, in May 1995, my lifelong friend and benefactor and Jackie's adoring husband died. I loved Oscar and I owe him everything.

Chapter Twenty-Three

The 1990s came in like a lion for Tramp. On 27 January 1990 we were a banner front-page headline in the *Evening Standard*.

RIVALS FOR THE HAND OF A LADY it read with, on either side, pictures of the editor of the *Sunday Times*, Andrew Neil, and the *Observer*, Donald Trelford, holding hands with the same Indian girl – although not at the same time!

'*Sunday Times* editor Andrew Neil told today how he fought to win the love of Commons call girl Pamella Bordes against the advances of rival editor Donald Trelford,' ran the first paragraph of a report from the High Court libel trial.

I'm afraid it was all my fault. Well, nearly all.

Andrew was a friend. I was pleased that in his entry for *Who's Who* where they have a section for clubs he put down Tramp, instead of the usual Garrick or Athenaeum (neither of which he belonged to). Rupert Murdoch made him editor of the *Sunday Times* when Andrew was 34 – a shrewd move. He courageously fought the battle of Wapping, defeating the dishonest practices of the print unions, and brought British newspapers (most of which criticised him at the time and all of which followed in his lead) into a new computer era. He also remodelled the paper after the *New York Sunday Times* so that its circulation wiped the floor with the opposition.

Pamella was an Indian girl, as exotic as the extra 'l' that she added to her name, who came to the club and, shall we say, made friends easily. She dressed expensively in Chanel, although nobody quite knew what she did for a living. I thought she came from a wealthy family.

She was a bit of raver, to put it mildly! She'd ask me, 'Who's this one and who's that one?' and then she'd be off and running. If somebody had said to me during that time that she was a hooker, I would have told them they were stark, staring mad.

I introduced her to Andrew. What could have been a fleeting friendship turned into a romance. And then Andrew's sister paper, the *News of the World*, decided to find out the source of her income: she charged by the hour – or by the night.

But not Andrew. Theirs seemed to me to be a genuine affair, not a financial transaction. This was not the opinion of the editor of the *Sunday Telegraph*, Peregrine Worsthorne, whose paper implied that Andrew knew that she was a prostitute, and further riled the young Scotsman with the suggestion that he wouldn't have found himself in this position if he had patronised clubs that were proper for his position – such as the Garrick or the Reform.

So Andrew sued him. The matter was complicated by the fact that Andrew, an unmarried man who could do what he liked in his personal life, found himself with a rival for Pamella in the improbable shape of the married family man, Donald Trelford.

The press loved it. Reports of the court case read like a comedy script. Worsthorne's counsel had asked Andrew to define a 'bimbo' and he replied that such a person was 'a very attractive young woman who wasn't terribly bright'.

Judge Michael Davies then examined the term 'ageing bimbette', which had appeared in an *Evening Standard* article about the affair.

'Surely it should be ageing bimbo rather than bimbette?' His Honour suggested.

Andrew replied, 'I'm not responsible for the quality of journalists on the *Evening Standard*, my Lord, but I think you're probably right.'

Although it was hardly pertinent to the case, Andrew was obliged to defend Tramp to Worsthorne's counsel, saying he had never seen drugs being taken there, had never met the Bay City Rollers or seen 'Bungalow' Bill Wiggins (an escort of Joan Collins).

'Tramp did not exploit in their publicity the fact that Miss Bordes went to the club. On the contrary, the management was rather troubled when revelations about her were published and to my knowledge she has not been to the club since.

'Since Tramp has members like Sir Clive Sinclair, Michael Caine and Frederick Forsyth and many businessmen and people from all walks of life leading perfectly respectable lives, I see no reason why I should change my opinion of it.'

Hear, hear!

Andrew won his libel case and was awarded a thousand pounds. Peregrine Worsthorne thought the damages were derisory: 'They would not even buy a man a weekend with Pamella Bordes.'

This was in part true, although for Andrew she came free – until she took her scissors to his suits.

Andrew, no longer at the helm at the *Sunday Times*, still comes to the club with his girlfriends.

Worsthorne is no longer editor of the *Sunday Telegraph*. I would like to thank him in print for giving us some amusing publicity more than twenty years after we were founded.

For a long time I was terribly naïve about hookers. Just recently a girl came back to Tramp who used to be in the club virtually every night and then vanished. She was sweet, pretty and very well spoken and used to come with her brother. They were from a good family. A reliable friend informed me, 'She's a working girl.' I was astounded.

One particular chap used to come into Tramp with the most beautiful girls, always American. I didn't find out until some years later that they were all hookers whom he would fly over from America.

Of course the famous ones were the Madame Claude girls from Paris – stunning girls who could be taken anywhere, to society affairs, the best hotels and restaurants, and would never be out of place. You would never dream that they were Madame Claude girls.

When Jan and I were on our honeymoon, we went to a club called the Papagayo in St Tropez. There was an extraordinarily attractive girl there, dressed in zipped leather, who was with a guy. I went to the loo and the guy followed me in. I became a little nervous, even more so when he said, 'I'd like to speak to you,' while I was having a pee!

'Yes?'

'You know the blonde lady I'm with? She finds you very attractive and she would like to be with you.'

I told him, 'I'm really flattered but I'm here on my honeymoon and I don't think my wife would quite understand.'

He persisted: 'Perhaps you could get away during the day.'

'Are you crazy? I'm sorry, but I'm on my honeymoon.'

'Please take my card.'

I didn't want to get into any more hassle, so I thanked him very much and took it.

He said, 'These are the telephone numbers where you can find her any time.'

I went back to our table, where Jan had been joined by two friends from London, Nigel Pollitzer, John Bentley (one of the first financial whiz kids) and a model called Mynah Bird, one of the fun girls from the sixties and seventies. Mynah went on to marry an African prince, but many years later she died in her apartment and tragically lay undiscovered for two months. Nigel, who was always fearless about chatting up girls, spotted the girl in zipped leather and the next thing I knew, he had invited her and her escort to the table. Jan and I left shortly afterwards, but the others stayed.

John Bentley fell madly in love with this girl and, later in the summer, brought her to the club. We talked and laughed about the night in St Tropez. The story had a tragic ending. She was, it transpired, a Madame Claude girl, and went to Saudi Arabia to earn some really big bucks. Unfortunately, she was caught and charged with adultery. The judge found her guilty and she was subsequently stoned to death.

Lady Rothermere, the wife of the proprietor of the *Daily Mail*, liked to end her evenings at the club, not always sober and frequently in the pursuit of pleasure. Bubbles, as she was known, had been a Rank starlet like Joan Collins but instead of waiting to become a star the beautiful Patricia Brooks made her fortune as Lady Harmsworth, when her husband became a viscount.

After the birth of their three children the Rothermeres seemed to live separate lives. I adored Bubbles – she may have put on a bit of weight since her Rank days but she had lost none of her sparkle. She would arrive in the club at two or three in the morning after doing the rounds of social events.

On one such occasion she turned up with a guy called John Gordon, whom she had picked up at some party. After a couple of glasses of champagne she suddenly noticed that her handbag was missing. She went berserk and accused him of taking it, whereupon he ran out of the club and down Jermyn Street, only to be tackled by her chauffeur. However, he didn't have the missing bag.

Bubbles, in a panic, phoned the police because she had lost her house keys. Two constables arrived and asked her if she wanted to charge Gordon. She was about to agree when I suggested to her that she first come into my office.

'Listen,' I warned her, 'if you charge him, what are you going to do? It's going to go to court. Can you imagine? It'll be in the papers:

Lord Rothermere's wife meets this man for the first time and brings him to Tramp, where he robs her. How's it going to look?'

'I don't care! The bastard deserves to get done,' she insisted.

So the cops took the guy down to the nick and said they wanted her to go, too. I felt I had to go with her to Vine Street Police Station.

My staff were still looking for her bag and I was truly fed up. I was tired, the publicity was going to be bad for the club as well as her and all I wanted to do was go to bed. So I asked the police, 'Can I go into the cell with this guy?'

The sergeant warned, 'Don't touch him!'

'I'm not going to touch him,' I protested.

But when I went into the cell I was furious. 'Now listen: I can get you out of this. All she wants are the keys to her house. Don't tell me you didn't take the bag, don't tell me you don't know where they are because I'll get pissed off. I'm not a policeman and I don't give a shit.'

He still denied taking the bag, but, before I found out whether my temper was going to land me in clink with him, Guido rang to say they'd found the keys behind the pipe in a loo.

I pleaded with Patricia not to charge him. She finally agreed at seven in the morning. I drove home in a foul mood.

So the story never came out. Until now. And it's too late to do her any harm because she died of an accidental overdose of sleeping pills in 1992. The following year her husband married his mistress, Joeong-shun Lee.

I miss Patricia. She lit up the club when she came in. I'm glad her son, Jonathan, is carrying on the family tradition – although not quite as excessively.

Talking of loos, at one stage I had all the lavatory lids at the club removed when it seemed that certain people were using them to lay out lines of cocaine and sniff them. This may have been *de rigueur* at LA dinner parties – I often witnessed it on people's coffee tables after dinner – but was not my style and not very good for my licence. People could put whatever they wanted inside them before they arrived, but what we offered them were just drinks.

Forget about drugs, this country has such antiquated licensing laws. They were brought into being in 1915 because of the chaps in the trenches – they didn't want them to think that everyone back home was getting pissed in the pubs or clubs. They've eased the laws, but they've never completely repealed them. There are still lots of stupid laws telling you that, at a certain hour, if you want to have a drink, you've got to eat. There shouldn't be any licensing laws. You see more drunks here than in France or in Italy, where they don't have any licensing laws. At present we have everybody suddenly coming out of the clubs at the same time – 3 a.m. – and the police getting mad because they're suddenly hit with thousands of people flooding into the streets.

In the early days of my club life, Easter was a very religious holiday. On Maundy Thursday – the one before Easter – you had to stop drinking at midnight. Then there was no drinking at all on Good Friday. But on Saturday you could drink until midnight. Then, again, on Easter Sunday, no alcohol. So after midnight on Thursday and Saturday we served orange juice and soft drinks and nonalcoholic beers. This was the law until about the mid-1990s. How much it placated God has never been recorded; although this was never an issue for the non-Christian drunks.

A guy from the Club Squad came charging down the stairs one Easter Saturday at exactly midnight and started to check the drinks. But he was out of luck: we had moved on to soft ones.

The same chap would come running down at one minute past three in the morning to make certain the bar was closed and nobody was being served a drink. And, at other times, at 3.30 a.m. to make certain there were no drinks on the tables. But there never were: my staff knew how to hold on to their jobs.

Nor did the spot checks on the lavatories to see if anybody was smoking or sniffing anything that was against the law ever yield any victims – one of which could have been my licence.

Chapter Twenty-Four

Any scandals or incidents that might take place in Tramp remained far from the public press. Nigel Dempster could probably have had a lead story every week, but he valued his membership and our friendship more than breaking the code.

One who did not was Piers Morgan, the editor of the *Mirror*. He used to have a column called 'Bizarre' in the *Sun* and he was a member of Tramp. Unlike Dempster, he was more interested in a good story than honouring the unwritten code of membership and in 1993 he wrote how at 4 a.m. (sic) in Tramp a drunken Charlie Sheen had asked him if he knew where he could get some blow 'to pep him up a bit'. Whether that's true or not, I wonder if anybody respects that sort of journalism. Charlie Sheen was welcome to come back to Tramp any time he liked. I told Piers he was out of order to print the story and that would be the last chance, otherwise it would be *au revoir*.

My own attitude to drugs was well known to members: if they wanted to fill themselves up with them, they should do so somewhere else.

But we are a club, not a court of law, and several people have passed through the portals who are perceived as less than perfect. Michael Winner, a good friend and celebrated film-director-cum-restaurant-critic, brought OJ Simpson in after his criminal acquittal and his less successful civil case.

OJ had been a founder member of Tramp LA. His amazing football career was over and he was making a good living advertising Hertz Cars and appearing in movies such as the *Naked Gun* trilogy. In fact he was dating the teenage beauty queen Nicole Brown (whom he later married) at the time and they were a very loving couple.

OJ looked well: still the same flashing white smile and crinkly smiling eyes. But he had to put on glasses to read the menu. Apparently he had spent sixteen months in solitary confinement on remand in an underlit cell reading books and it had ruined his eyesight. And, he said, his golf game had been harmed because his knees had gone: doctors wanted to replace his right knee and he had already had six operations on his left one.

He wanted me to know that he was sleeping with Nicole right up to the time he is said to have murdered her. I'm not a judge but I must say he certainly convinced me; if he did it then he's the world's greatest actor.

As we sat at the table he was hit on by girls so incessantly that we barely had time to talk. This came as no surprise to him. 'I get more offers from women now than I ever did as an all-American hero. Just shows women go for a dangerous dude. Or maybe they believe – like the jury – that I'm not dangerous.'

Michael Douglas, while between marriages, just loved Tramp. To say he had a wandering eye would be an understatement. In February of 1998 he dropped by when I had Martine McCutcheon and another actress, who will be nameless, from *EastEnders* for a drink. Michael joined us and charmed both women.

The following day he rang me and said that he rather liked the soap star and suggested we all have dinner. So I rang Martine and asked her if she would like to come to the Bluebird restaurant for dinner with Jan and me and Michael.

She was thrilled by the idea and Michael later said how great he found Martine.

After dinner he suggested we go to Tramp but it was too early. So I said we could go to the Met bar for a drink first and then to the club. But Jan had to get up early, so I took her home and met them at the bar. They decided not to go to Tramp because Martine had to go to the East End and Michael had an early call.

The following Wednesday the front-page headline in the *Mirror* revealed TIFF'S FATAL ATTRACTION with a picture of Michael and Martine (Tiffany in *EastEnders*) leaving the bar. It correctly reported: 'Oscar-winner Douglas had been introduced to Martine by his nightclub boss pal Johnny Gold at the week-end.' But the rest was the usual mix of fact and fantasy, pointing out to readers their age difference – he was 53, she was 21 – and repeating the canard that he had been to a clinic that specialised in sex addiction. So what was a simple friendly evening out was turned into the passionate match of the moment. Don't believe everything you read in the papers.

Incidentally, I adore Martine and am delighted she has achieved such heights of stardom. She is brilliant in *My Fair Lady*.

For the first two decades at Tramp, I had continued to run my bookmaking business from my office with three staff. Several members, not least George Best, liked to avail themselves of the service, but it was increasingly hard.

All went well and profitably until 1991, when Satellite Information Services (SIS) came into being, and bookmaking was suddenly covering horse and dog racing from all over the world. In the old days there'd be a half-hour interval, or at least fifteen minutes, but now there were no intervals. I was tired as it was, trying to run that business in the afternoon and Tramp at night. I was going to bed at 5 a.m. and sleeping for six hours at most. So, with regret, we called it a day and I made sure my colleagues were well looked after and I passed on my customers to Victor Chandler, England's best bookmaker, a fine gentleman and a good friend. I still miss the thrill of it – but not the hours.

However, Satan finds some challenging tasks for idle hands to do and, when the Belvedere restaurant in Holland Park in west London went bust, I had a hunch I could make a go of it.

Holland Park used to be privately owned by Lord Ilchester, but his Jacobean mansion was bombed during the war and is now largely a youth hostel. The spacious outbuildings were turned into a restaurant by the Joe Lyons group, famed for its comfortable surroundings and terrible food. They used to say it was like a canteen for the directors of Lyons.

Ten years ago it had been bought by a catering company owned by a Swiss businessman, Dieter Apt (who subsequently became a good friend). He had spent a lot of money refurbishing the Belvedere. But the company went into liquidation. So Bill Ofner and I bought it off the receiver for a considerably smaller amount of money than the place actually was worth.

It was still a major gamble, but it turned out to be pretty good for us. We changed things around to how it had been before Dieter put in his wavy wall and decorated the walls with the brilliant celebrity photographs of Terry O'Neill. We got quite a lot of publicity through Tramp and through members of Tramp eating there and telling their friends it was not a club and was open to all. I think the Belvedere was arguably in the best setting of any restaurant in London. I loved going there – sitting out on the terrace in the summer listening to the peacocks and watching John Cleese and Iain Johnstone sitting at their regular balcony table writing the script of some movie.

Michael Winner used to tell me, 'Darling, you're the only person who could have put the Belvedere on the map.' Which we did – it was a cause for considerable satisfaction.

Chapter Twenty-Five

Princess Diana never came to Tramp. But she nearly did. Twice.

The first occasion was in 1983 when she, Sarah Ferguson (not yet married to Prince Andrew) and Billy Connolly's wife, Pamela Stephenson, decided to go out on a London hen night.

They dressed up as policewomen and the plan was to raid Tramp. Their car drew up outside and Sarah sent down the driver to make sure I was there. Unfortunately, I wasn't – so they went to Annabel's instead. I spoke to Diana subsequently at Sarah's wedding party and she said she thought that their scam would have been much more fun at Tramp.

The second occasion was many years later. One of our most stylish members, Sanjay Hinduja, asked me if Jan and I would like to come up to dinner one night at the family home in St James's. His father would like to meet me. I said it would be a privilege. His family was known to be one of the three richest in Britain.

What followed was a little bit of a mix-up. Sanjay said he thought next Wednesday was the day of the dinner but he would confirm it by the weekend. As he hadn't, Jan and I arranged to have dinner at the Belvedere with our friends Chris and Mickey Most (the record producer).

Then Sanjay rang on Monday confirming the Wednesday. I was in a bit of a spot: we had stood up the Mosts on two or three occasions because of work and no way could we do so again. So – great British compromise. Jan would eat with the Mosts and I would join them after going up to the Hindujas.

When I walked into the Hindujas' palatial pad, I could immediately see it was a fairly formal gathering. As Sanjay introduced me to Gopichand (his father) and Srichand (his uncle), I could see there were about thirty people there and the only white faces were mine and Princess Diana's.

She and I had spoken only briefly before but now we had a really good chat and a lot of laughs. She was fabulous. I levelled with her that I had to join my wife at dinner and she teased: 'You mean to say you're going to stand me up and not be my date tonight?'

I said, 'I tell you what, why don't you come to Tramp afterwards? I'll see you at midnight at Tramp. Shall I come back to pick you up?'

But she pleaded she had to get up early the next morning. I stayed to listen, spellbound, to her speak to the assembled Asians about the plight of lepers and later learnt from Sanjay that she raised nearly half a million pounds that night alone. Not many people in the world could do that.

I didn't see Diana again but I did see a lot of Dodi, who kindly gave my son, Nicky, a terrific boost to his career by having him experience all manner of jobs at the Ritz in Paris – including working at reception, where many Tramp members were surprised to encounter him. When she saw him in his black jacket and striped trousers, Joan Collins threw her arms around him and screamed, 'Nicky, what on earth are you doing here?' – somewhat to the amazement of the rather stiff French managerial staff.

Dodi used to phone me all the time, more so when he began his affair with Diana. He knew Jan and I were going to the Colombe d'Or in late August and we agreed to have dinner with him and Diana.

I was driving home the Saturday before the planned meal, when my mobile rang. It was Dodi.

'Johnny, where are you?'

'I'm driving past Lord's cricket ground – where are you?'

'I'm in St Tropez, we're meant to be having dinner tonight with my friend' – he always referred to Diana on the phone as 'my friend'.

'Dodi, it's next Saturday, not this Saturday, next Saturday.'

He said, 'Oh shit, that's the day we're leaving. Tell you what, though. We could make it for lunch at the Colombe d'Or that day. Will you be there in time?'

I told him we would, and he apologised for the mix-up in dates – I should mention that such mix-ups were not unusual for Dodi. But the following Thursday his secretary, Annabel, called me and said, 'Johnny, Dodi just phoned and said would you please make certain you keep your mobile on on Friday because he wants to phone you to make arrangements for Saturday?'

I said, 'Fine, no problem. Give him my love.'

But I never spoke to him again. He and Diana returned early to Paris. Jan and I went as planned to the Colombe d'Or. At two o'clock on the Sunday morning I got a phone call from Terry O'Neill.

'Johnny, have you heard the news?'

'What?'

'Dodi and Diana have been in a crash in Paris. They say that Dodi's dead.'

I was half asleep. 'He can't be. Don't be silly, it must be the bodyguard. You've made a mistake, go back to bed.'

About three hours later the phone went again. This time it was Jackie Collins phoning from LA. She told us that they were both dead.

I got out of the bed and put on my swimming trunks. Our room was right by the pool. I just swam up and down, up and down, as the day dawned. But not for them. I had had so many happy, funny times with Dodi, and so had Jan.

*

Oscar was dead, Bill Ofner was very ill and I was about to get my bus pass, so, when Kevin Doyle's company, Caledonian Heritable Ltd, approached us not long before the turn of the century to buy both Tramp and the Belvedere, it proved to be an offer we couldn't refuse. Sadly, Bill died just after the deal was completed. As I have written earlier, he was a man of fortitude and compassion and vision – even if he did love to buy second-hand kitchen equipment. I miss him greatly.

We didn't want a lot of publicity about the sale. Kevin reckoned that the shareholding in the club was of no relevance to the members, just to the management. It is still good to be involved with the company, especially with Kevin and his wife June and his partner, Graham Arnott, and his wife, Janice. Brian Crawford, director of operations for the company, has done a formidable job. I genuinely enjoy working with him. We have a few different ideas – I was shocked when he wanted flowers in the club. But I guess he was right: the punters seem to like them.

I'm proud of my children: they're both in the business. Claire has passed her Higher Certificate in Wine and is now going for her Diploma in Wine. She works for Coburn and Campbell, who supply wine to restaurants and bars and clubs, and you'd be crazy to deal with anyone else.

In one of life's inexplicable coincidences, Nicky is now general manager in exactly the same premises where I started off in the club business. Then it was called Dollys, now it is 57 Jermyn Street. I hope he has as much luck as I did. He's certainly on the right track.

Without the paperwork of my club or restaurant or, indeed, bookmaking business to occupy the day, I have managed to improve my golf game to the extent that I am no longer a danger to other players on the course. I have done this with my dearest friend, Errol Brown of Hot Chocolate fame. Errol was a cult in the seventies and renewed his success in the nineties when the hit film *The Full Monty* used his song, 'You Sexy Thing', as its theme.

His talent is terrific but what really pisses me off about him is that his golf game is going better than mine. Recently he and Ginette, his delicious wife, went with Jan and I on a golfing trip. I think Errol managed to win the cost of their whole holiday from me in bets. Luckily, I had a couple of winners on the race track, thanks to Michael Tabor, who phoned to tick me up with them.

I remain a danger to myself on the racecourse. I adore racing and the thrill of a bet. However, it has been my good fortune to go to Ascot and the Derby and the Arc de Triomphe and even the Kentucky Derby in the company of my good friend Michael Tabor, who has a nice knack of winning races, so my losses have been limited somewhat.

Michael, like me, started out as a bookmaker but now has become a top owner. Thanks to him I have been in the most sanctified places on racecourses that I had only previously dreamt about – or seen on television. Michael and his partner, John Magnier, have treated me as though I were part of their team, now arguably the most powerful and successful in the racing world.

I have walked the courses with them and their inspired young trainer, Aidan O'Brien, and their gifted jockey, Mick Kinane. The hospitality in their boxes hosted by their groomed and glamorous wives, Doreen Tabor and Sue Magnier, is something to die for; in fact I sometimes feel I *am* about to die, after eating and drinking to lavish excess. But I shall always be grateful to them, especially to Michael, for enhancing the joys of my life to such a level.

I share my passion for racing with Maurice Menasseh, who played cricket for Oxford and Middlesex and is now an investment broker. His son, David, inherited his love of sport and is a successful sports agent with about a hundred and twenty footballers on his books. Maurice tends to drive me to the races, either he or Michael White, the theatre producer whose *Rocky*

Horror Show has been running longer than my clubs. Both of them take pity on me and take the wheel to stop my bones getting too weary.

Michael Tabor has a business partner, JP McManus, who arranged a special game of golf at Limerick. Michael whisked me there in a private jet in the summer of 2001 and we had the privilege of walking the course with JP and his opponent, whom many would see as quite a challenge – Tiger Woods. Under a complicated Irish handicapping system, JP managed to beat the champ 5 and 4.

It was just magnificent to watch the golfing genius close up and receive the occasional tip. At the eleventh he put his drive into a seemingly unplayable position beneath some bushes. Most players would have taken a drop or a second drive. Not Tiger. He got down on his knees and played a perfect shot to the green.

'You play better on your knees than I do standing up,' I told him.

'Ever think of having your legs shortened?' he quipped, smiling. And what a smile and what a charming guy.

Every Thursday, when possible, I attend the lunch meeting of the Mayfair Orphans. This is one of Britain's smaller clubs originally consisting of only five members: Sir Michael Caine, Terry O'Neill, Doug Hayward, Philip Kingsley and me. The underlying qualification for membership is to be an orphan, which we all are. Philip, the noted trichologist, was merely an associate member for many years until his 99-year-old mother died two years ago. We have had another new member, Mickey Most, since the sad loss of his mum.

Philip maintains the club grew out of a sixties football team called the Mount Street Marchers. Michael says it originated in a conversation in Doug's club when we all realised that our parents were no longer alive. Terry said it began over lunch at Langan's, where we used to eat every Thursday, and decided to institutionalise the custom.

So, as you can tell, we have had plenty to argue about over the past thirty years. When we began fine wines would flow; now that we are a little older and more careful with our waistlines and livers, it tends to be mineral water. The Orphans has a strong overseas membership list, at the head of which is Roger Moore.

One of the pleasures of my position was to watch other people's fortunes flourish over the years. Robert and Vincent Tchenguiz, twenty-year stalwarts, started out with a million between them but built up a multimillion-pound conglomerate of properties, pubs and oil refineries.

Laurence Stroll, the owner of Ralph Lauren Europe, didn't know anybody when he came to London; now he is the sixth richest man in Canada. He bought Tommy Hilfiger and floated it and recently acquired Aspreys. In a profile of him he was asked to list who had influenced him most and I was flattered to come in fourth.

Phillip Green was selling cut-price designer clothes in a shop in Conduit Street when I first met him. Recently he joined Jan and me for lunch.

'Do anything today, Philip?' Jan asked.

'Not much,' he replied. 'I just bought British Home Stores.'

For his wife's fiftieth birthday he organised a surprise birthday party in St Tropez. Sadly I told him we couldn't make it: I was in the middle of business negotiations and just couldn't spare the time.

But Philip didn't get to the top by taking no for an answer. 'How about I send a car for you on Tuesday at noon. There will be a private jet at Northolt and helicopter waiting at Nice to take you to the garden of your hotel in St Tropez. You have three-quarters of an hour to relax and a limousine will then bring you to the party. The following day a helicopter will take you back to Nice and the plane will have you back in England by three. How's that?'

'That's great,' I said. 'How about the spending money?'

Another trip we won't readily forget was as guests of David Tang, the Hong Kong entrepreneur. He took forty of us to China, laying on lunch (not a picnic but tables laid with linen and crockery) beside the Great Wall with a band and tango dancers. The guests included Rolf and Marianne Sachs, Lord and Lady Weinberg, Richard Curtis and his brother-in-law, Matthew Freud, Eric Wachmeister and Parmesch, a wealthy Indian woman who was also a Tramp member.

The following night David arranged a banquet in the People's Assembly Room, which is normally available only to foreign delegations. Then we went to the Chinese Opera. Afterwards David announced we were going to a club. Silas, his partner, introduced us to the manager who led us through a succession of corridors, past rooms with Chinese girls in long traditional dress.

After several minutes, the manager stopped and instructed all the women to enter one room and all the men the next one. Ours had a huge cinema screen with images of Superman, Godzilla and Buck Rogers projected on it and opposite it a bar and luxurious banquettes. The door opened and ten young Chinese girls marched in and stood to attention. They looked as if they were awaiting execution. But Silas asked us to pick a number from one to ten. I chose four, the ugliest one, who seemed quite grateful as perhaps nobody had ever chosen her before. She sat down beside me and offered me a song book. Although she spoke no English, she pointed to a page as another girl sang 'My Way' into a karaoke machine. An English-speaking girl, much prettier, sat on the other side of me and placed her hand on my thigh. 'Soon we go upstairs and you can do what you like,' she informed me.

But the door flew open and a man summoned Lord Weinberg, Mr Rolf Sachs and Mr John Gold as their wives wanted them. Needless to say, we left immediately. On the way home Jan told me of their experience. They had been provided with young Chinese boys in Armani suits who offered them a similar menu:

'Do you want chewy-chewy or fucky-fucky?' It may have been traditional Chinese hospitality but they didn't want to find out!

I watched Jackie Collins' hard-working rise to fame just as Tramp itself was starting off. Two years after Oscar died she fell in love with an old friend, Frank Calcagnini, and they travelled the world together. Tragically, he died, also of cancer, in April 2000. Jackie is far from alone: she has three smashing children – Tracy, Tiffany and Rory. But earlier this year she asked Jan to go with her on a book tour that included Warsaw, Sofia, Budapest and Prague to promote *Lethal Seduction*. It was so gruelling that the girls ended up in Paris for a bit of rest and recuperation. Jackie remains the dearest friend of all our family.

The good thing about working nights is that I have been able to enjoy both my family and my home, where we have had some memorable nights with our friends Norma Hayman the producer, Pat Booth with her late husband Garth, Michael and Glynis Brandon, as well as the usual suspects I've mentioned before. Our house – near Abbey Road Studios – was built in 1850 and described by John Betjeman as unique. It had been intended as a sort of folly, built by the man next door as an annexe for his daughter. But she didn't like living there, so he ended up letting it to a priest who devoted his life to saving fallen women. Sometimes they became a bit more fallen when they fell under his care, like the one he made pregnant.

Bram Stoker, sitting in the garden and looking up at the rounded Gothic windows, is said to have found his inspiration for the novel *Dracula*. Thackeray and Dickens were frequent visitors for literary debates.

I doubt that my book quite lives up to the quality of their prose but, there again, they weren't in the nightclub business. Which I intend to be until they have to carry me down Tramp's stairs.

And now, if you will excuse me, I have to go and take Max for his walk.

Index